# Animal Mandala Adult Coloring Book Vol 1

## 60 Entertaining Stress Relieving Animal Patterns

By Omar Johnson

I0486671

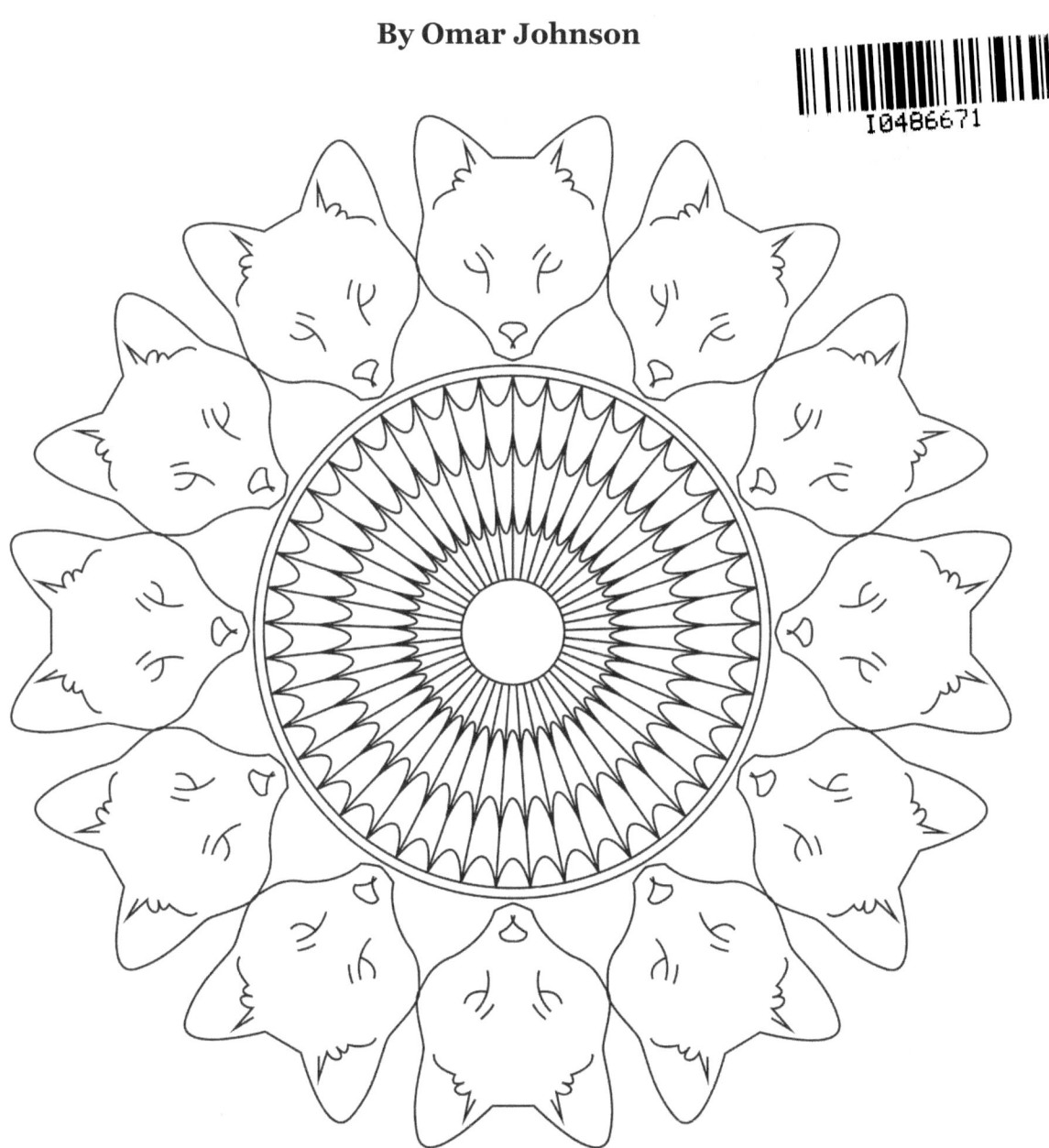

# Get Your Free Mandala

## Visit

## ADULTCOLORINGBOOKSFORYOU.COM

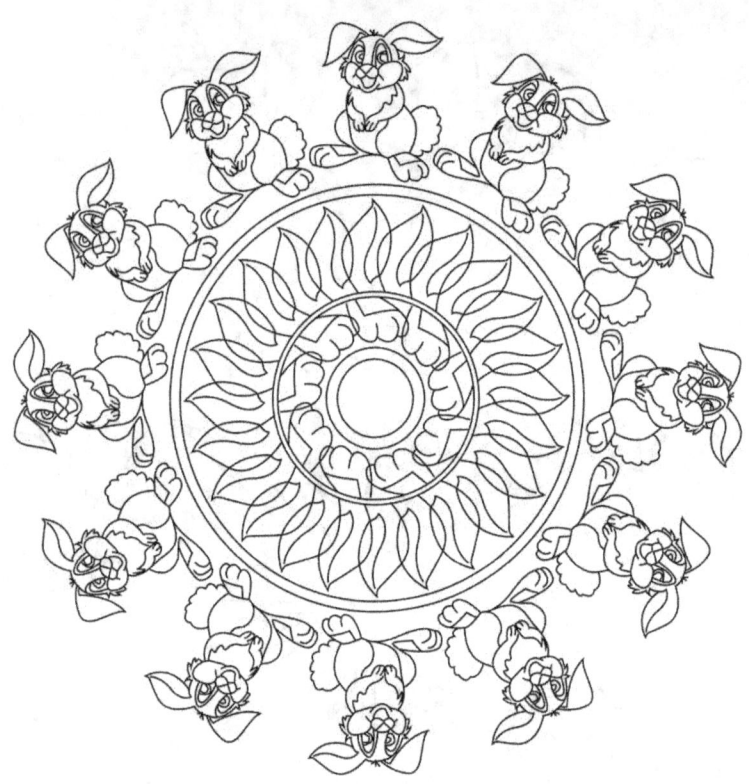

*Make Profits Easy LLC Publishing*
profitsdaily123@aol.com
Copyright 2015

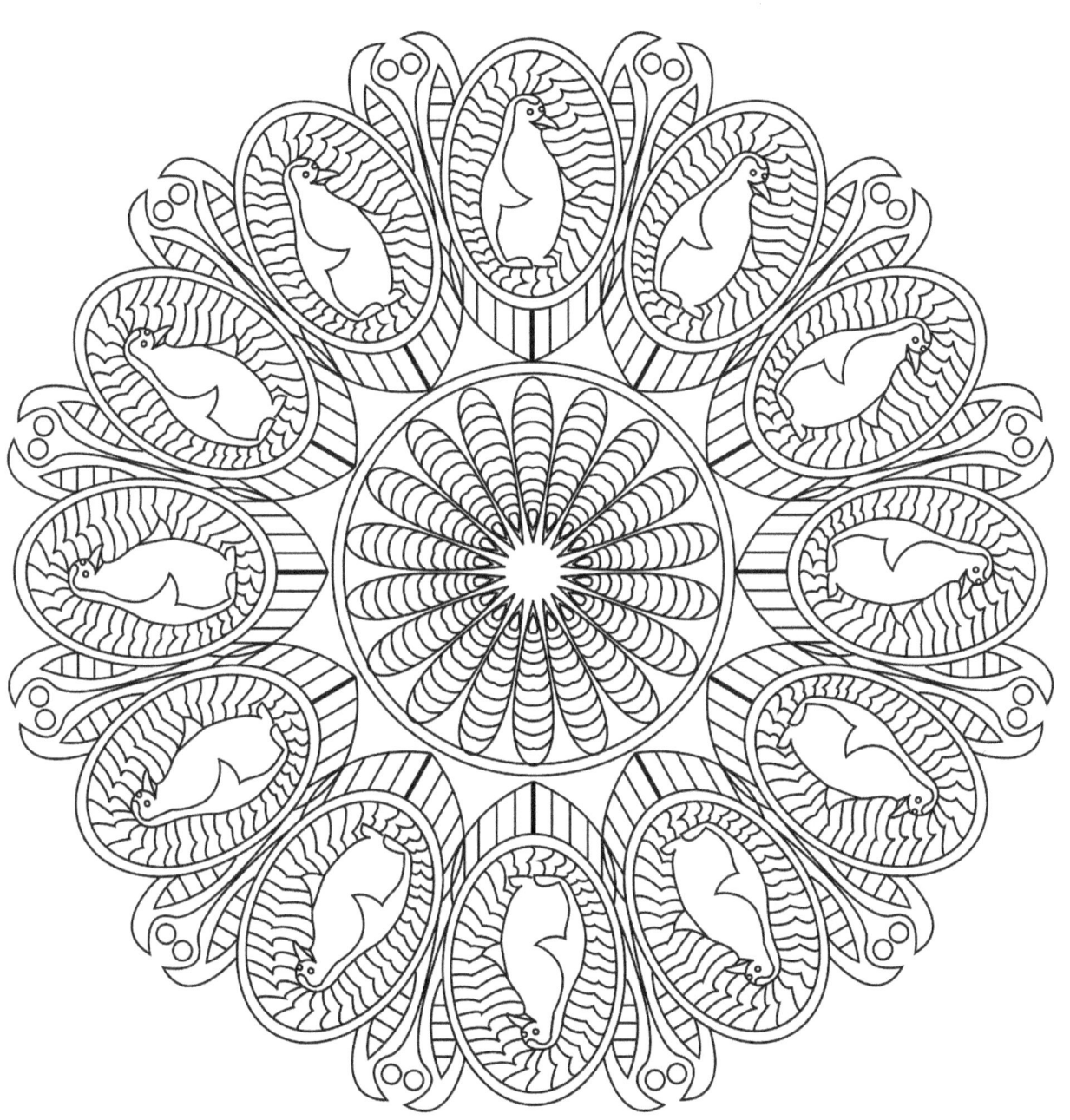

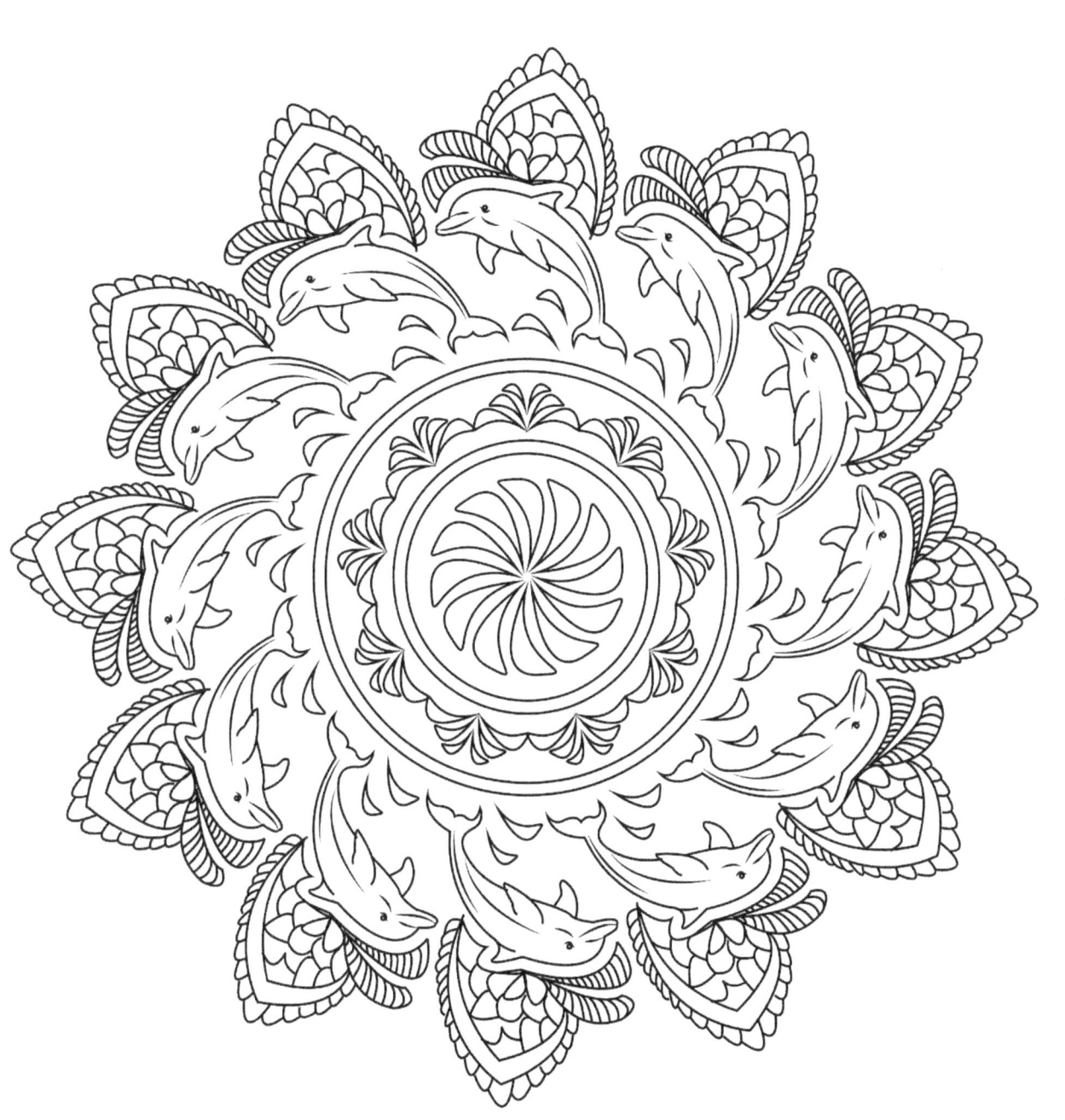

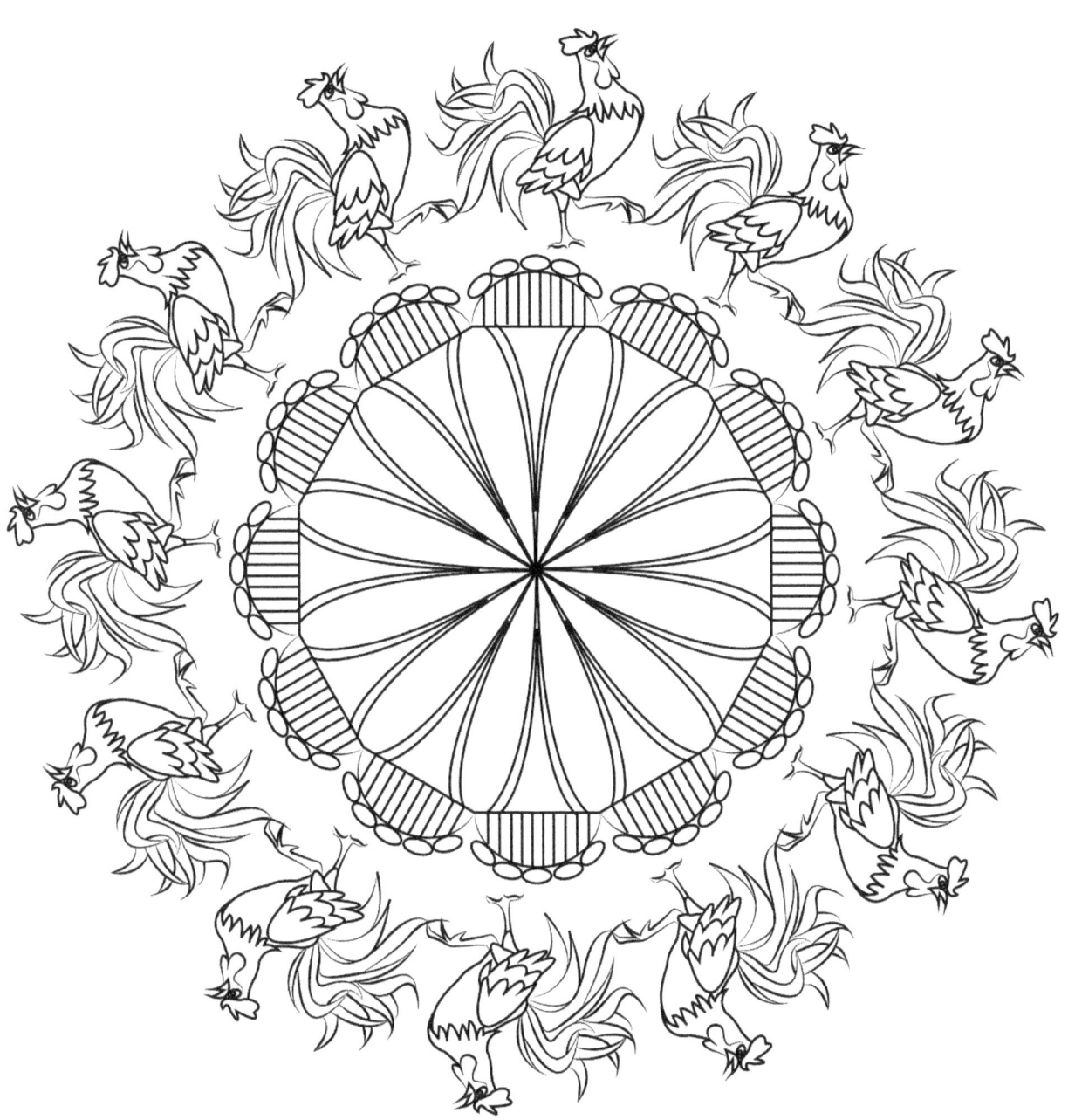

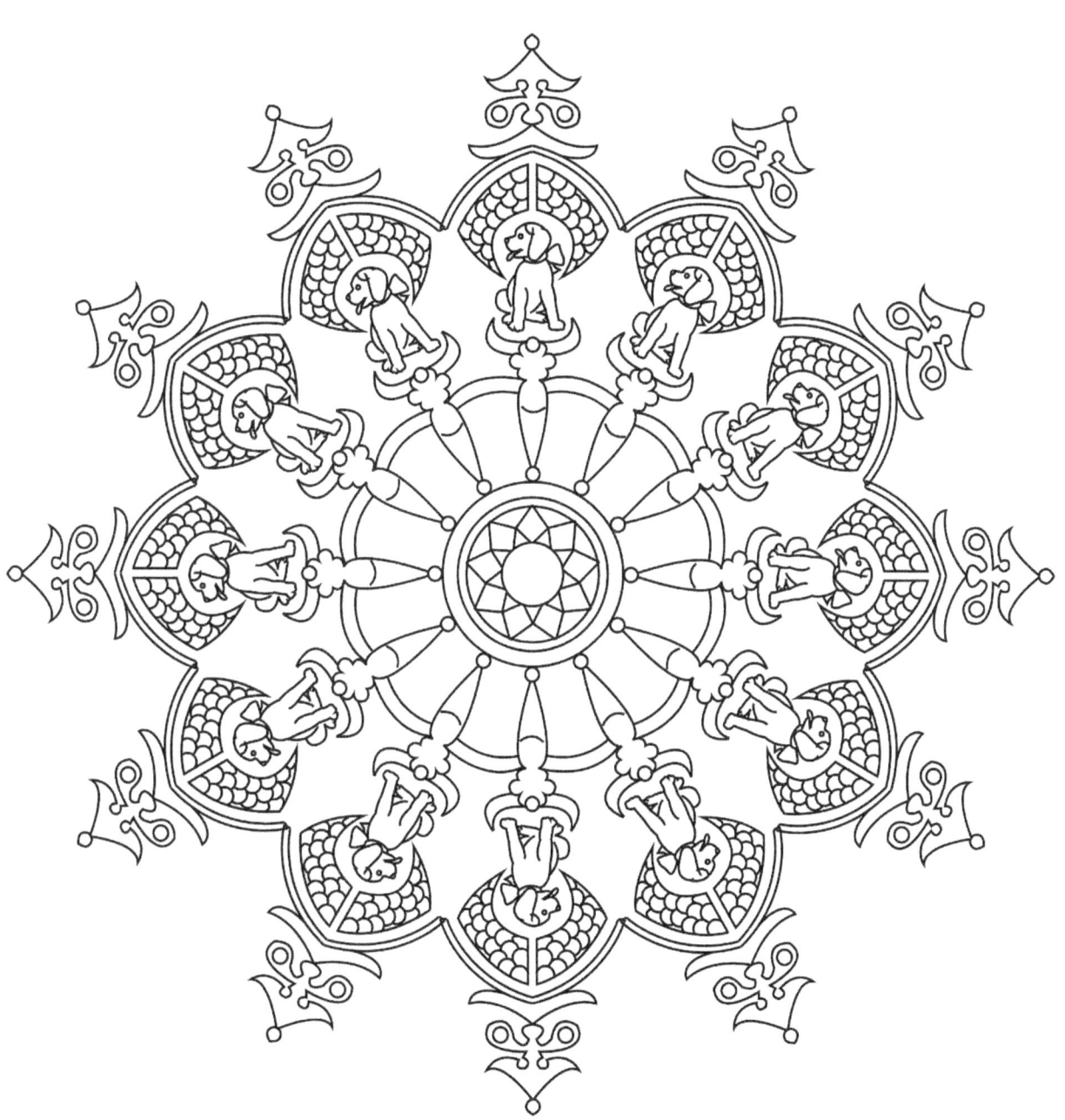

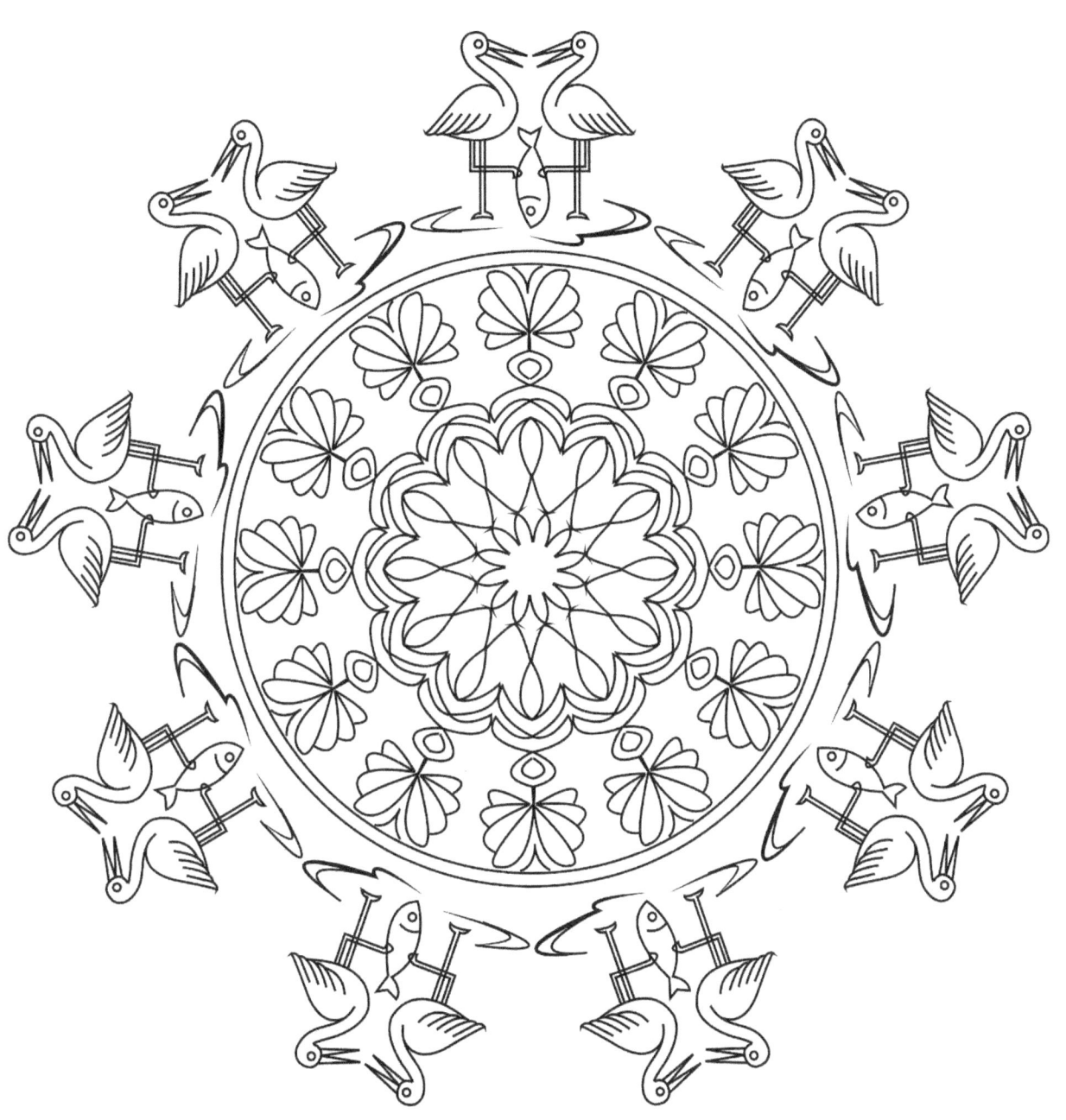

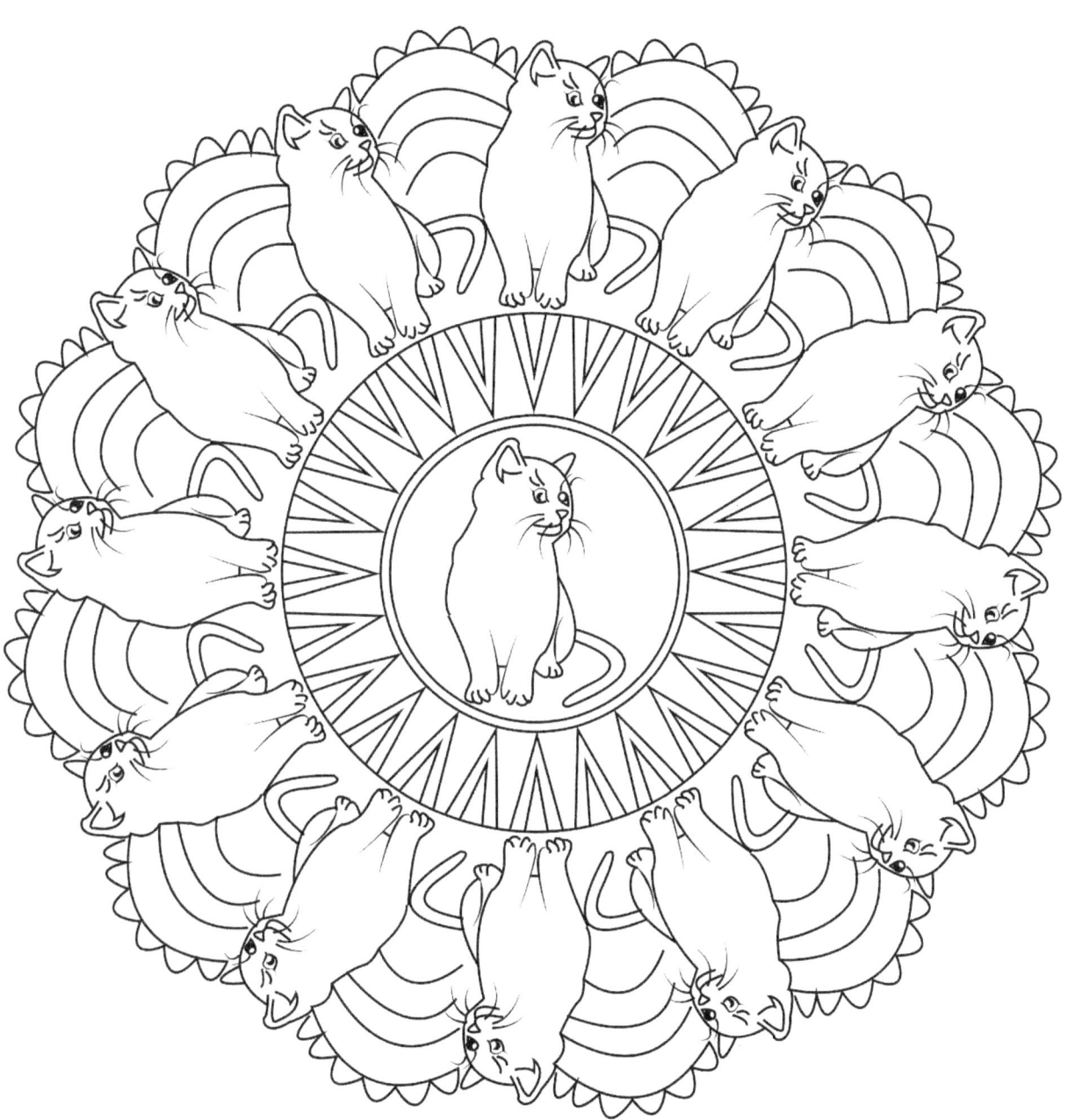

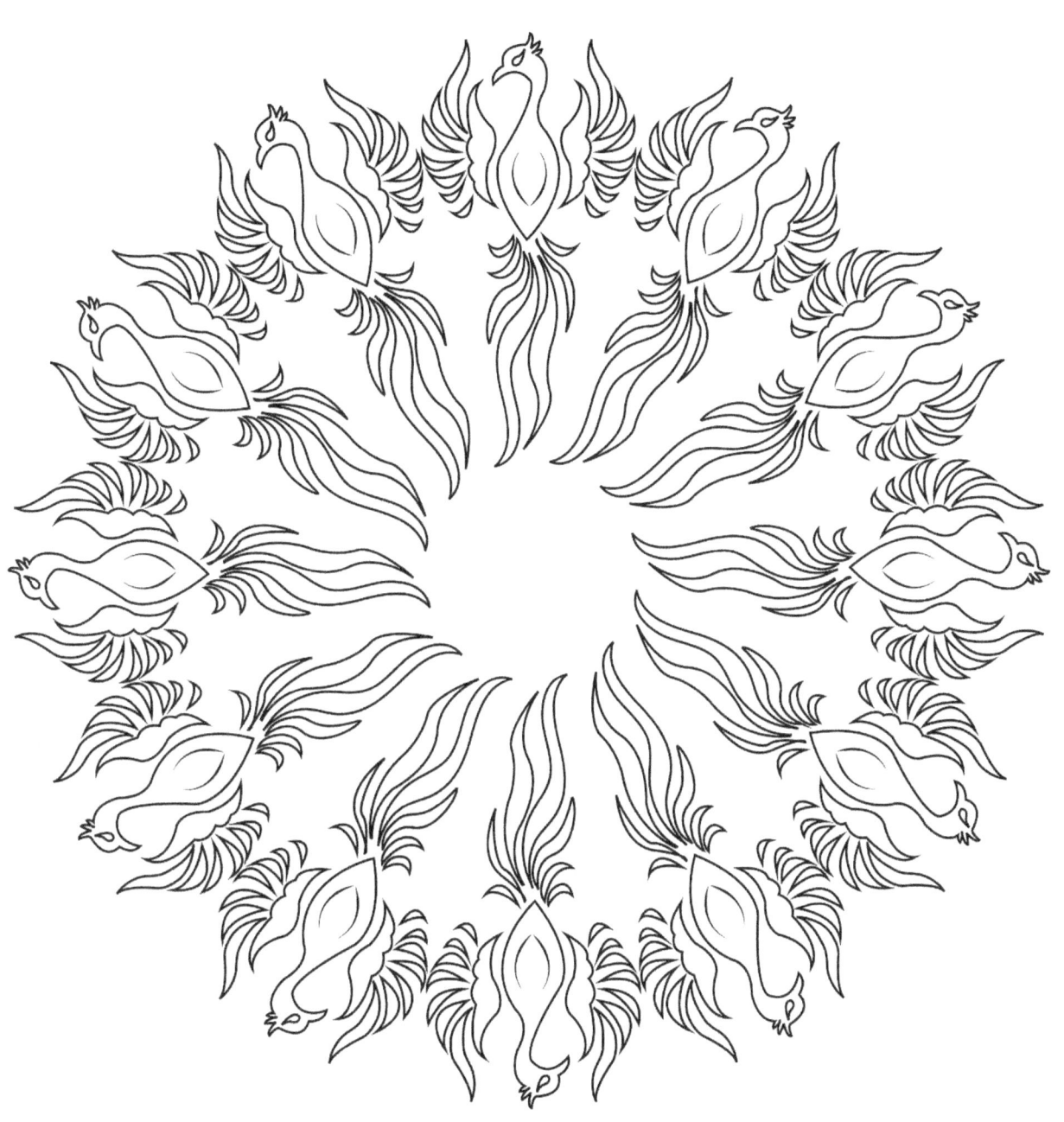

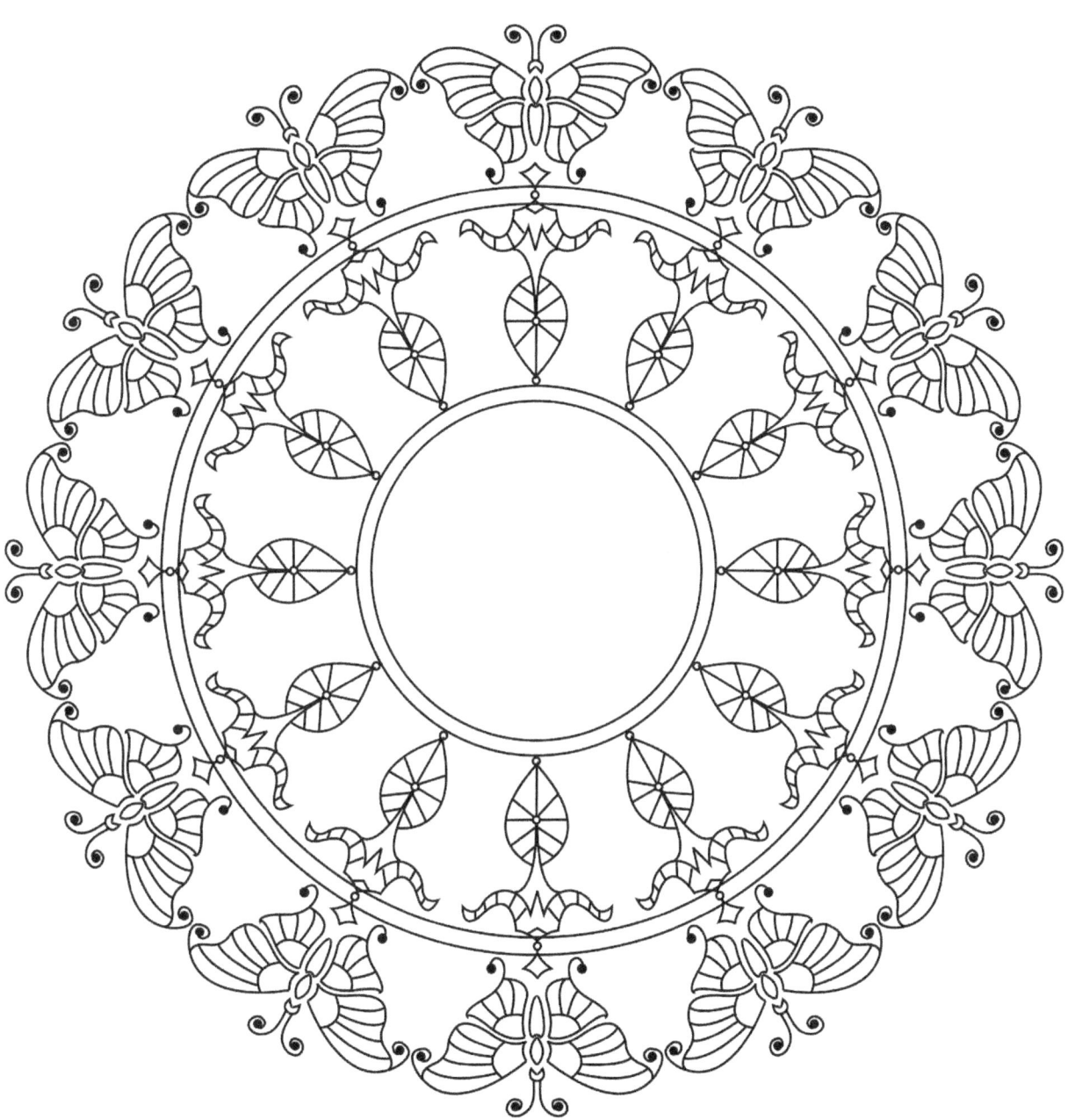

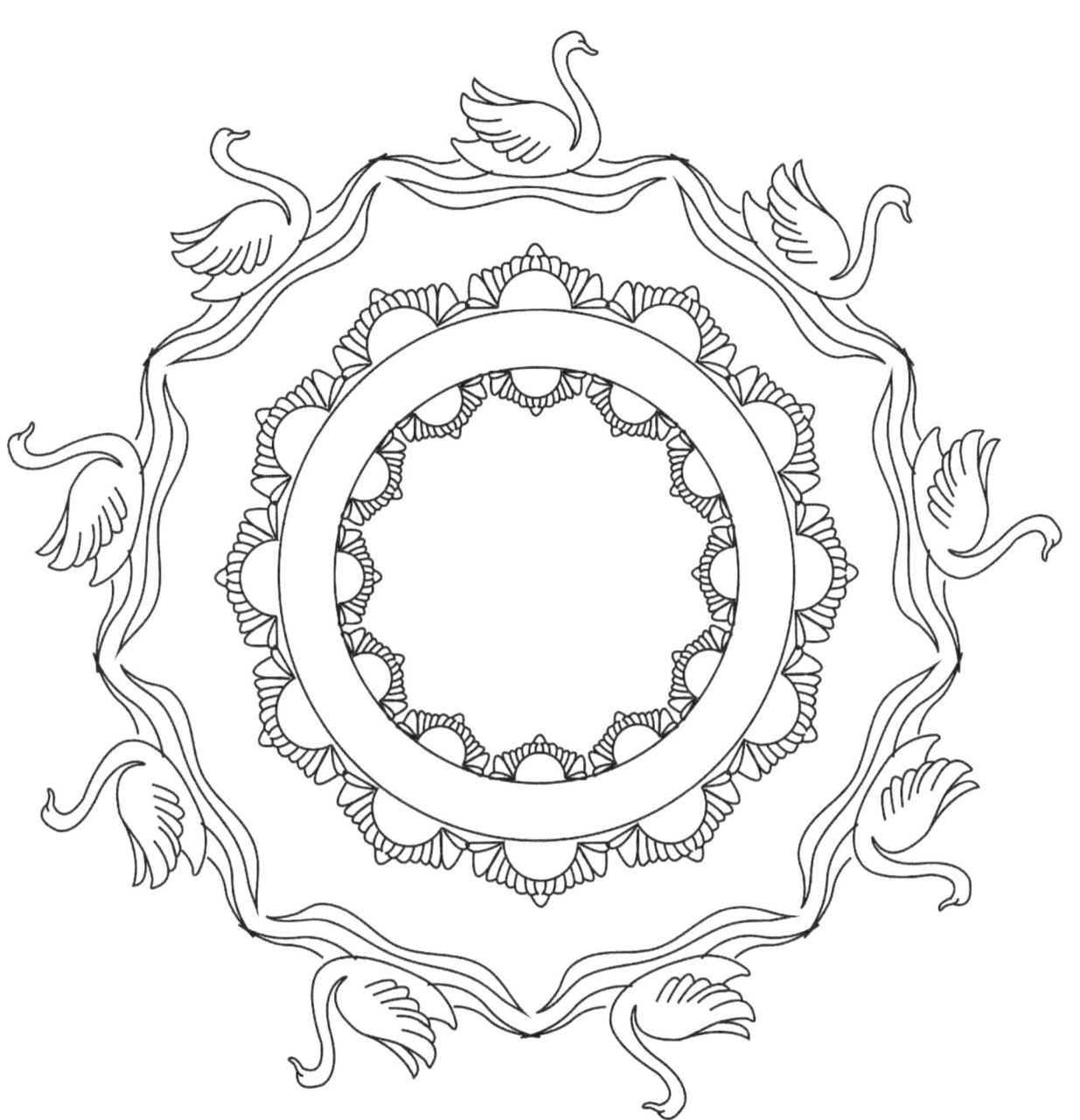

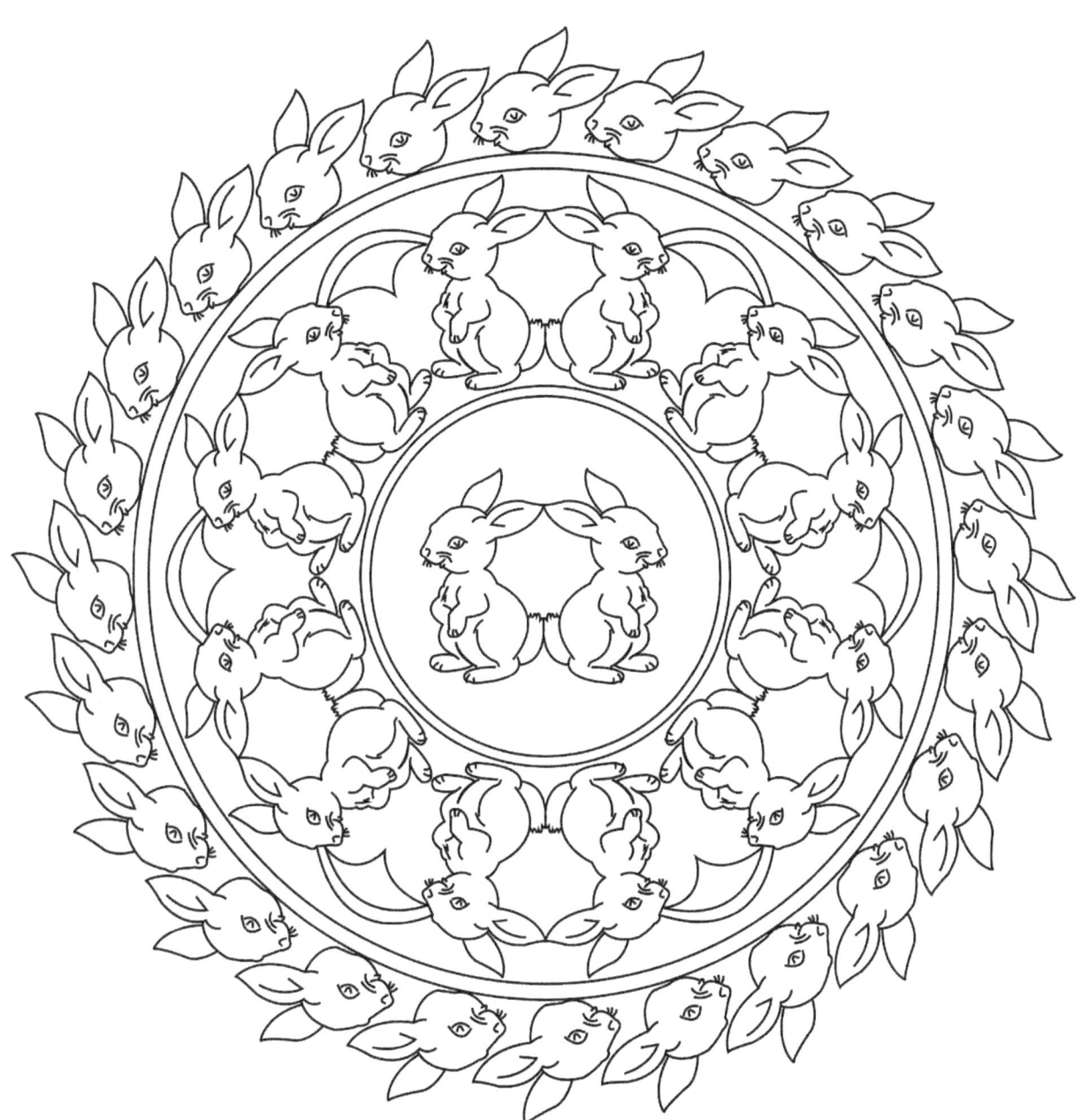

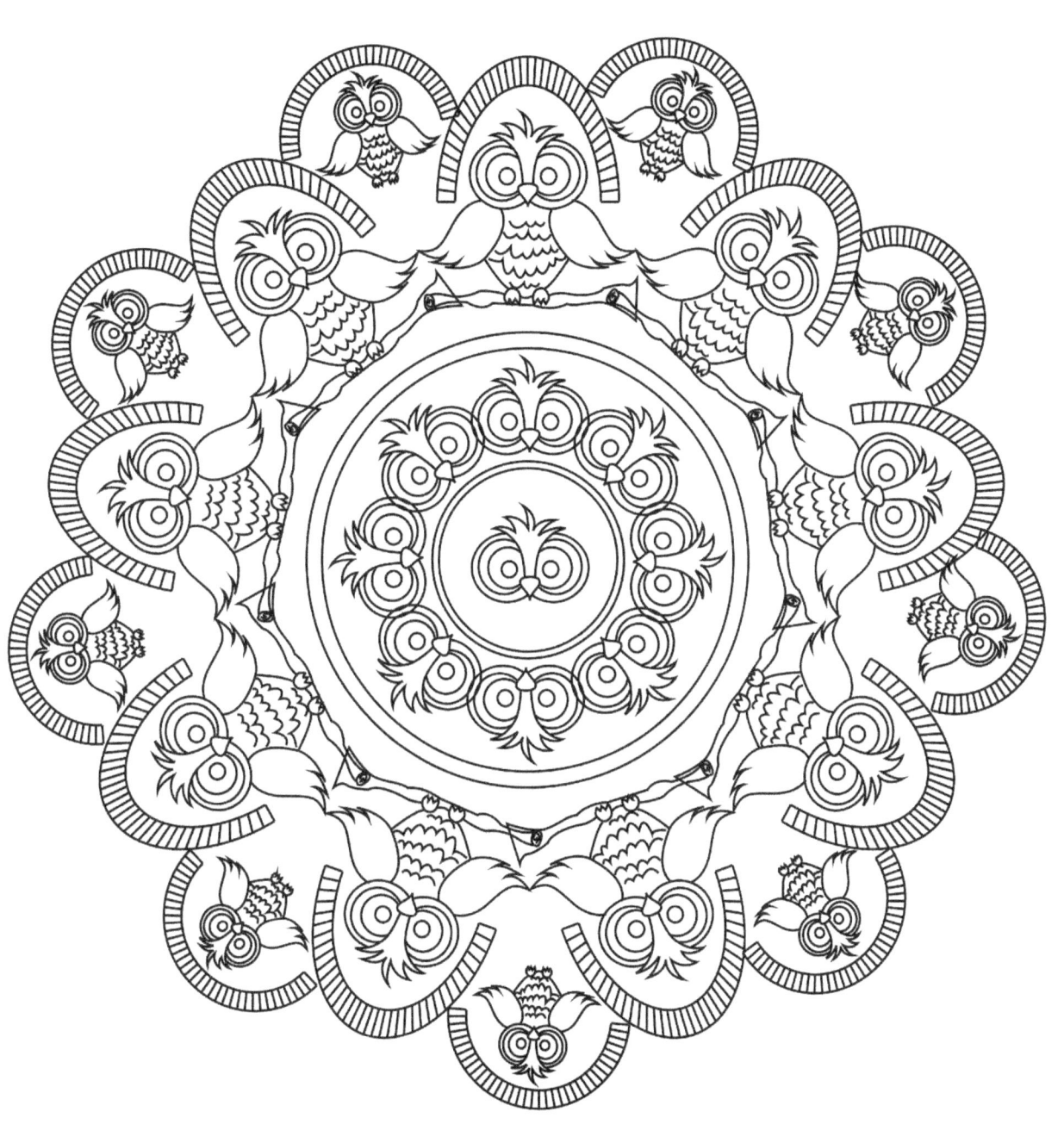

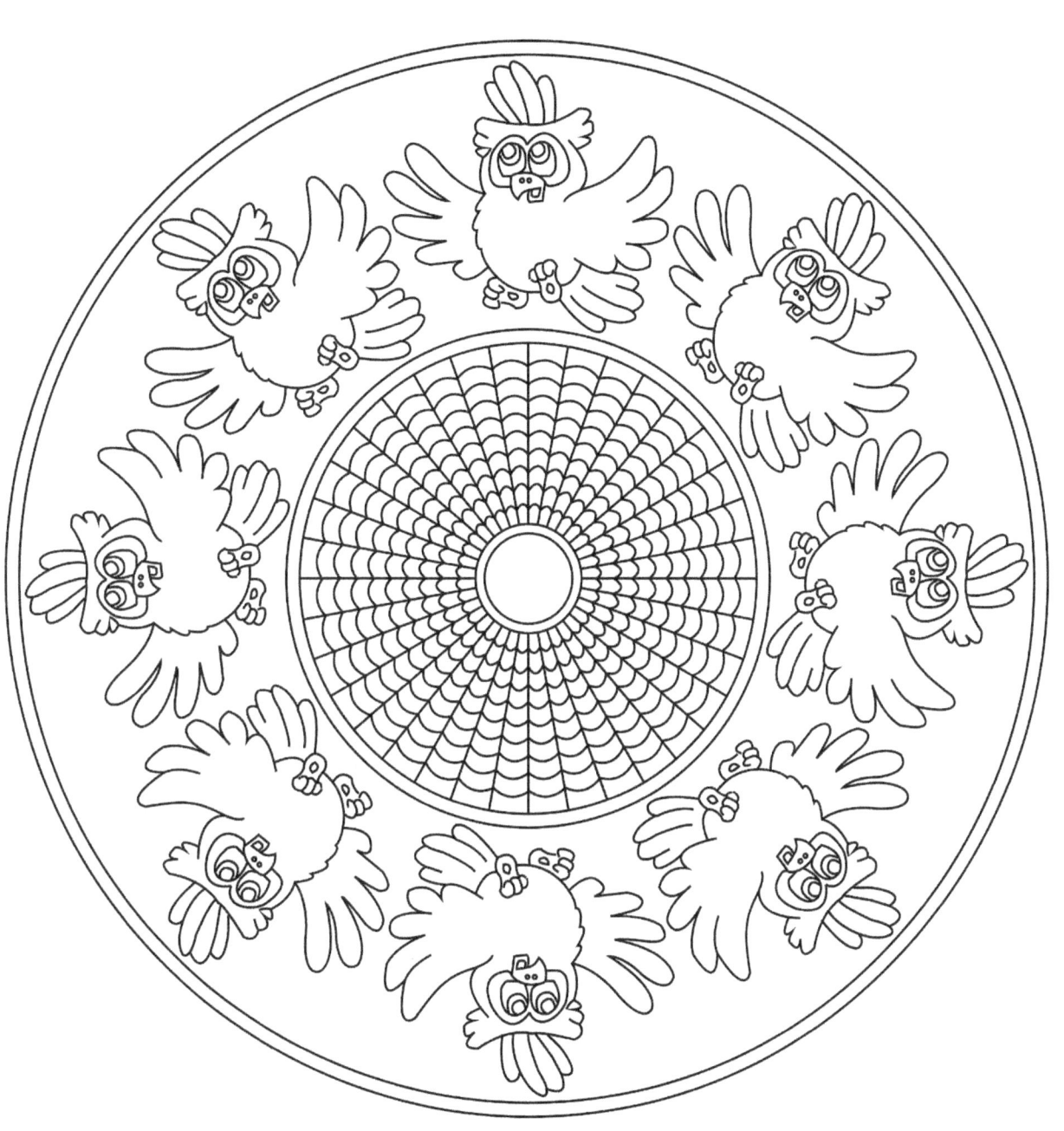

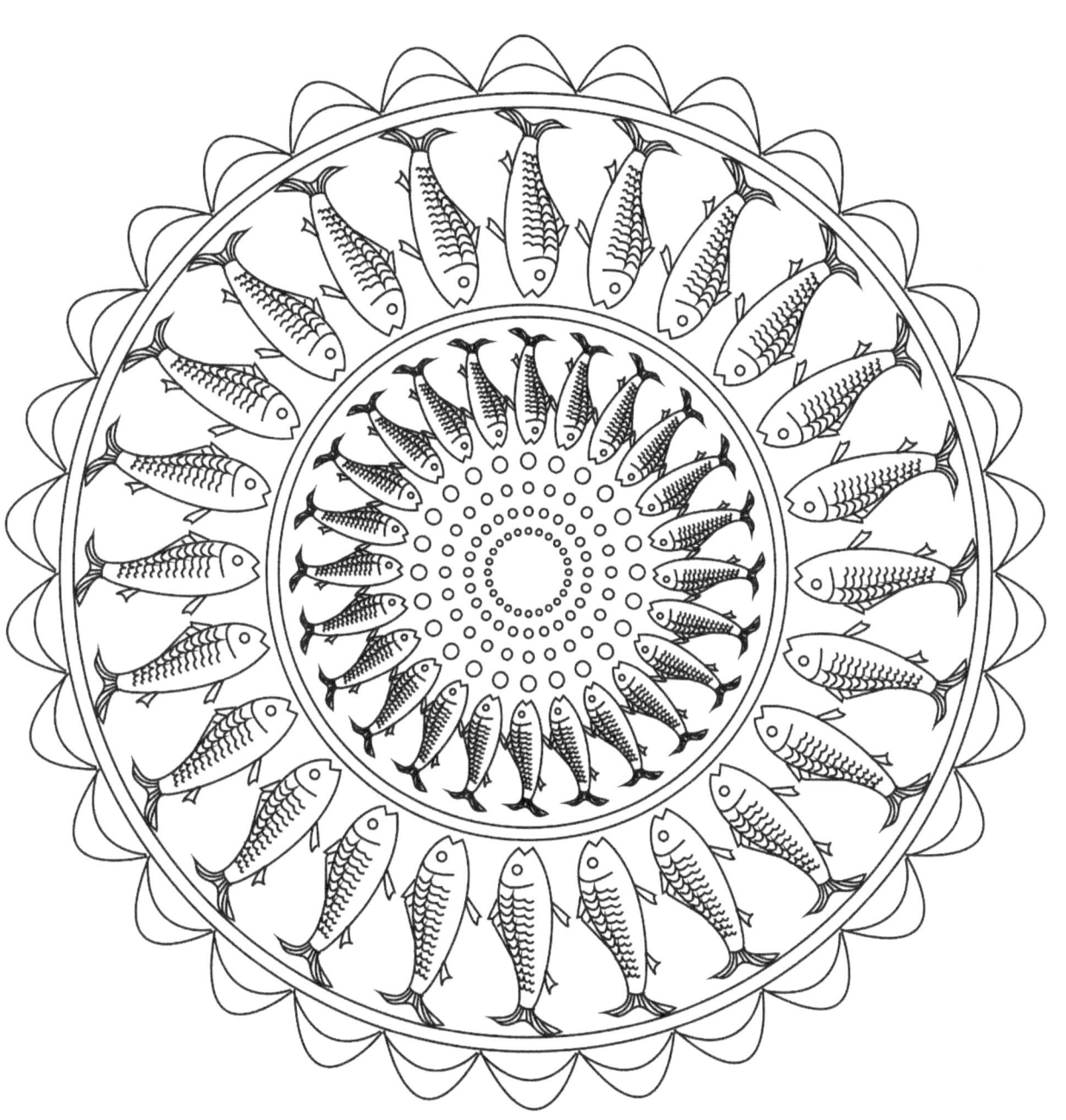

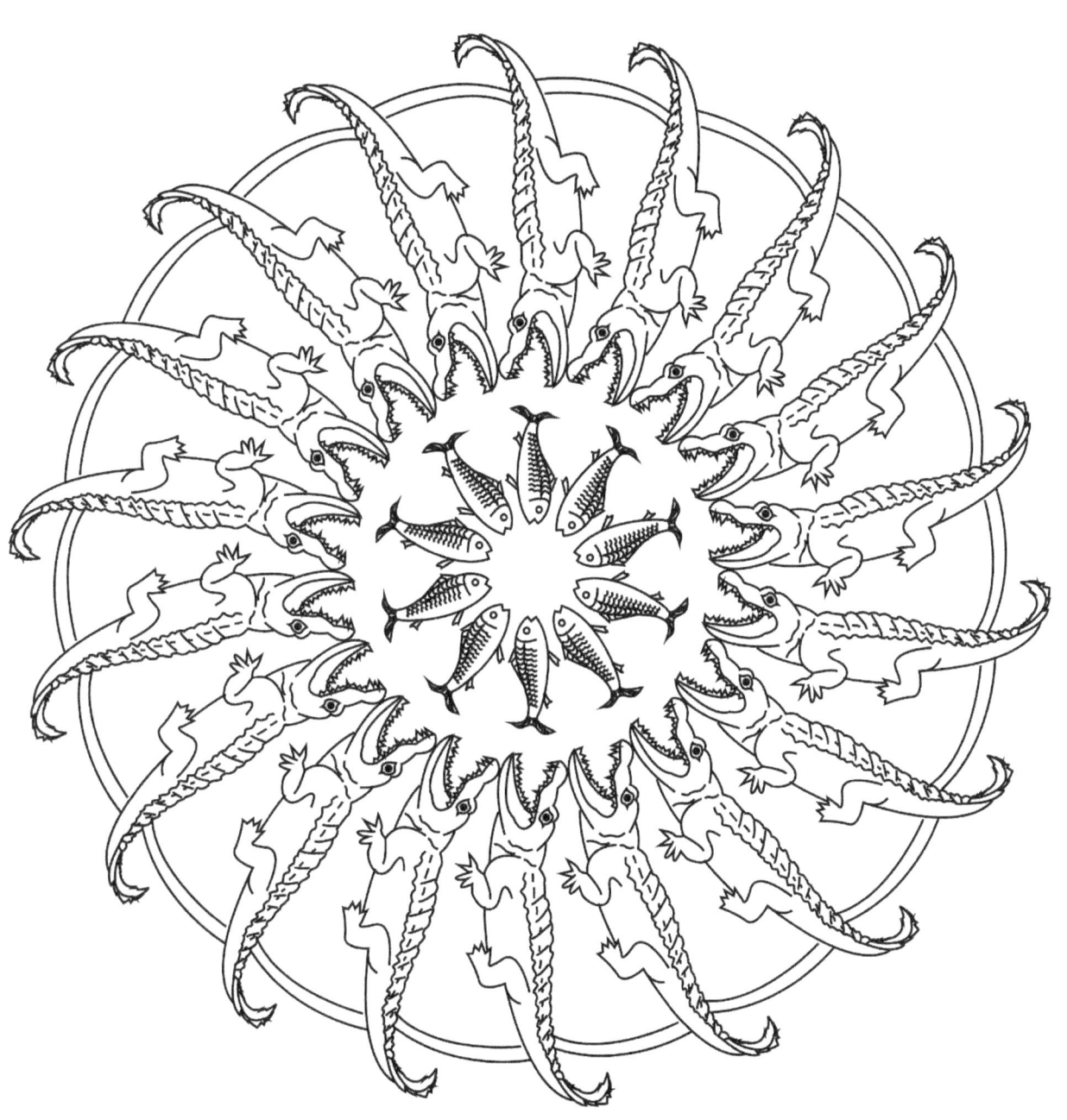

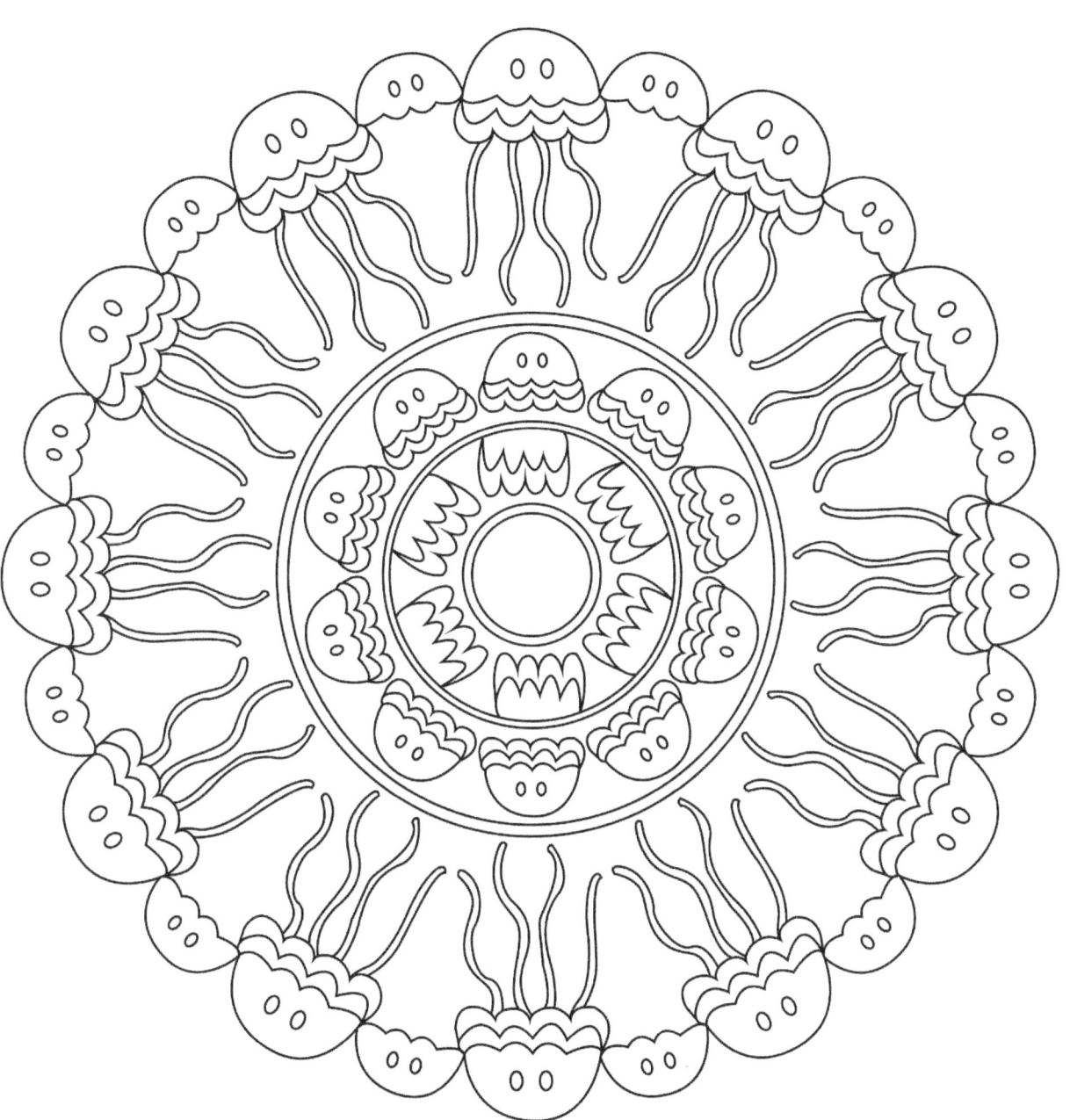

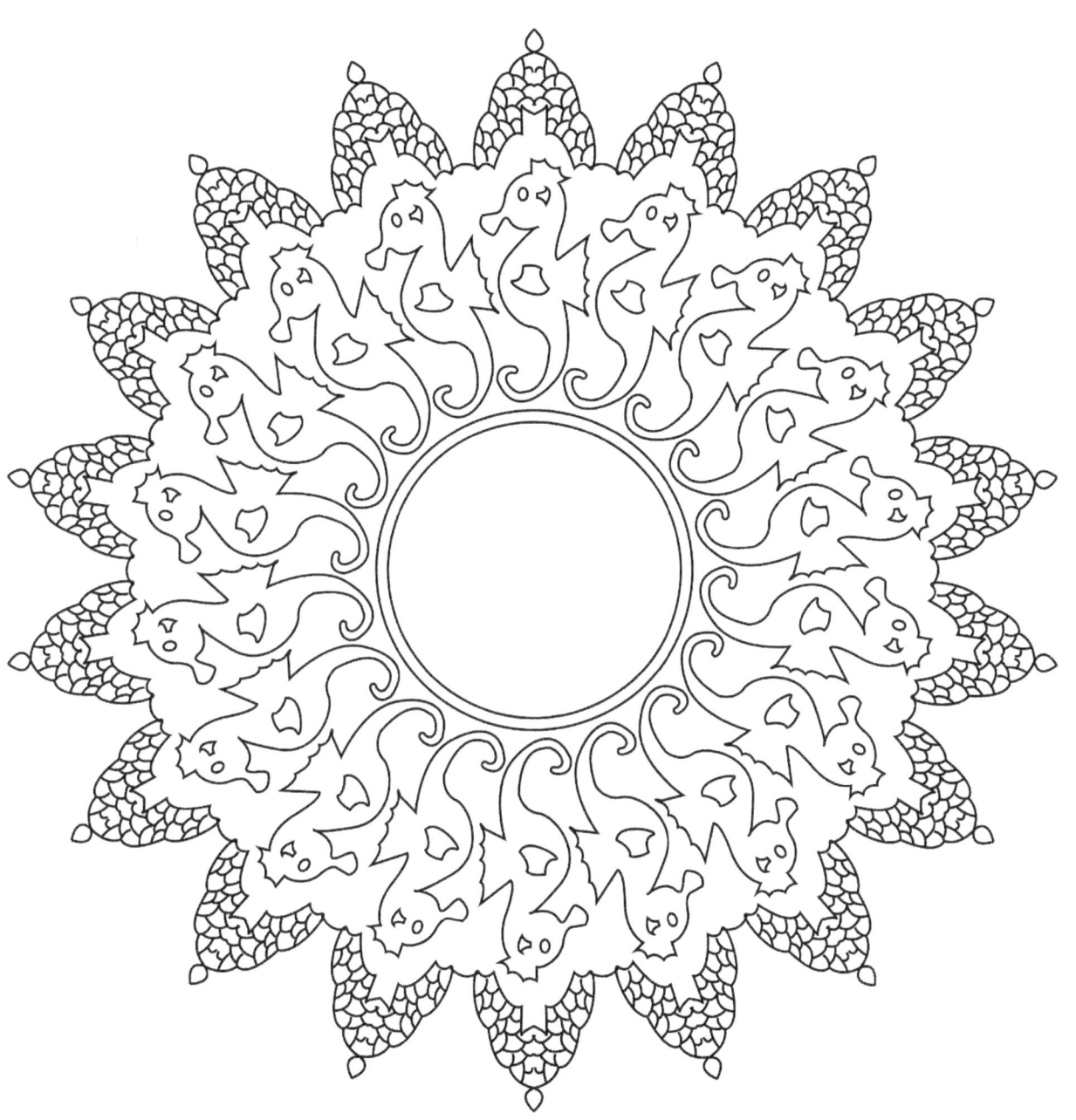

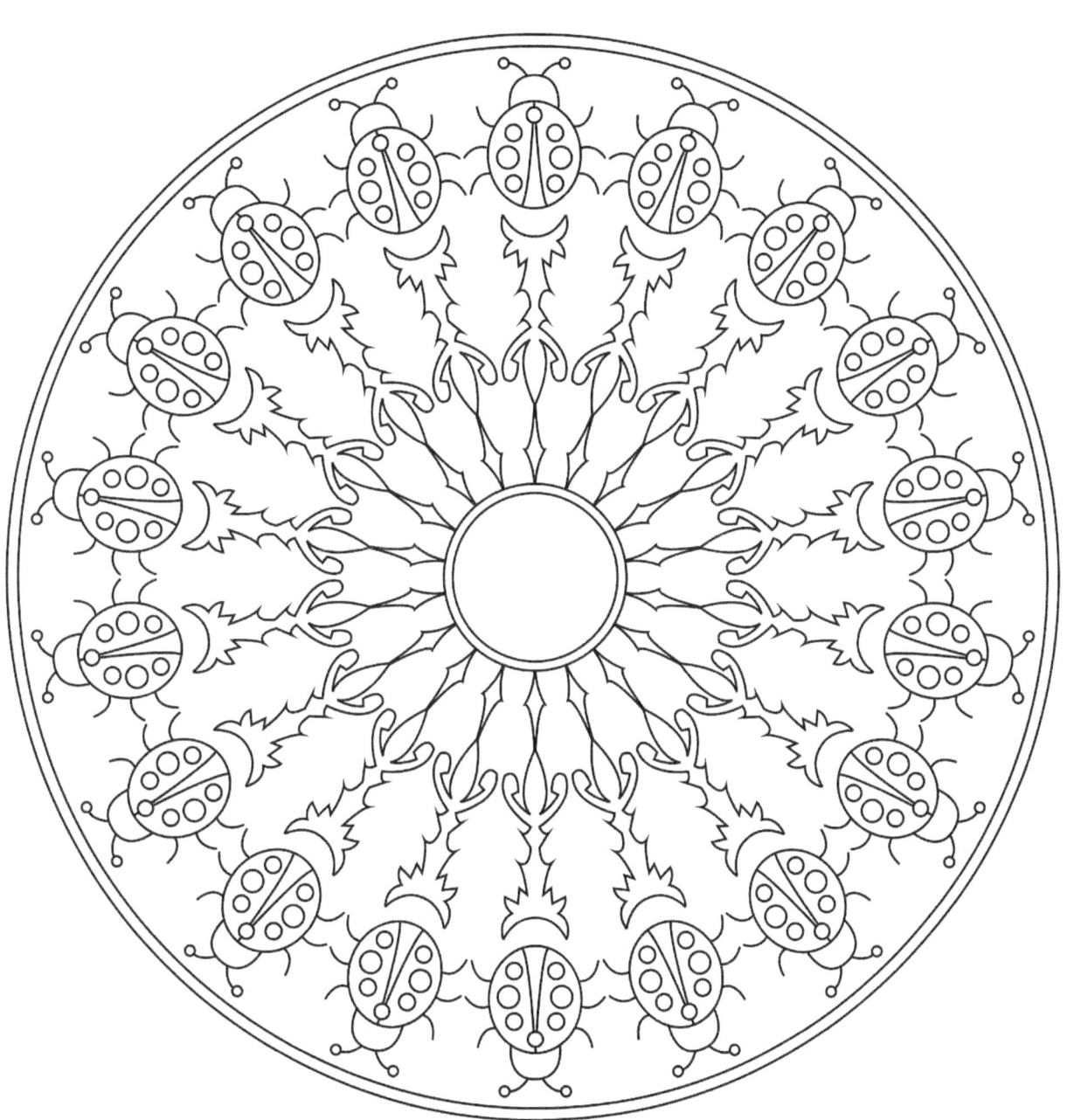

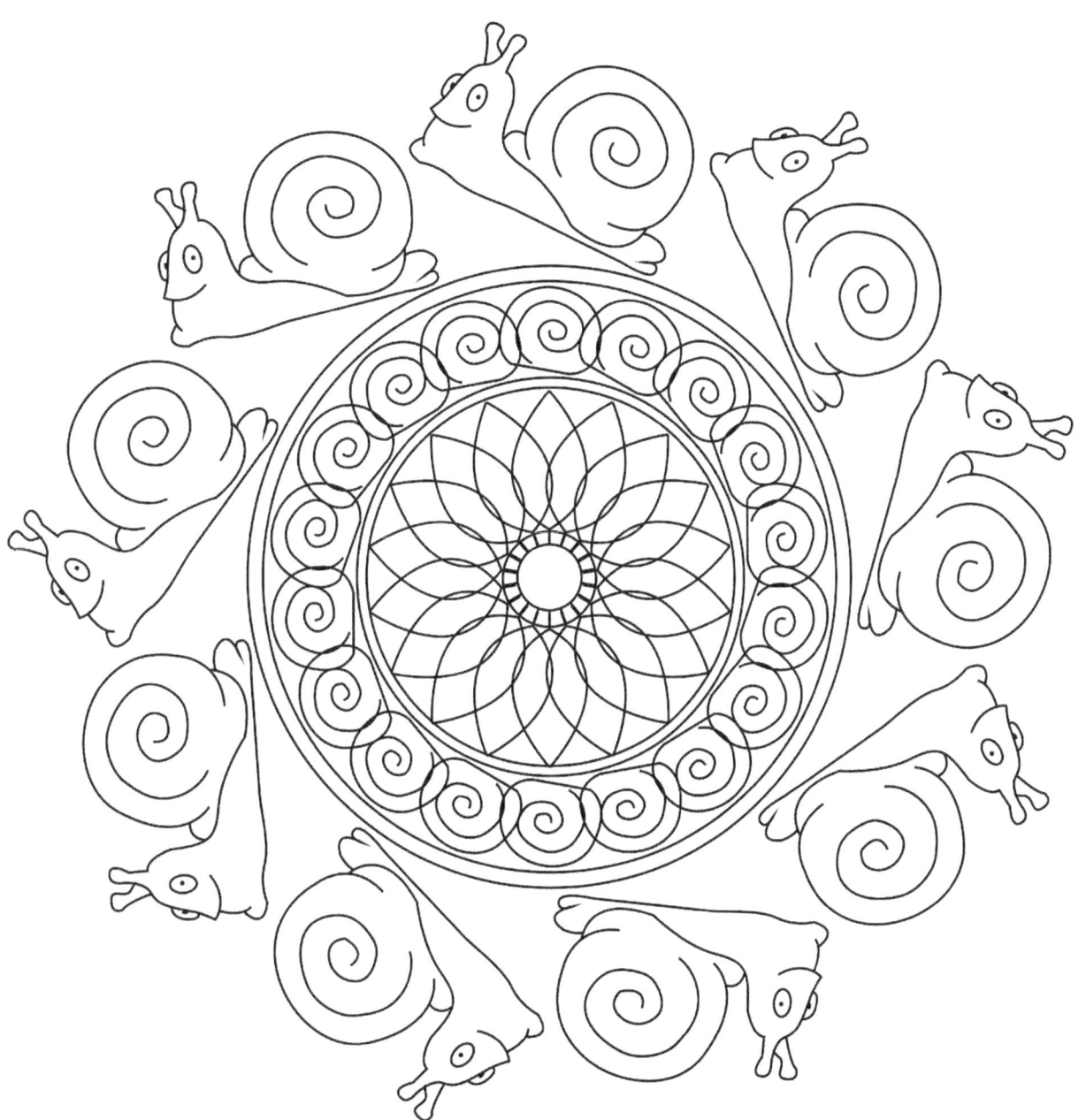

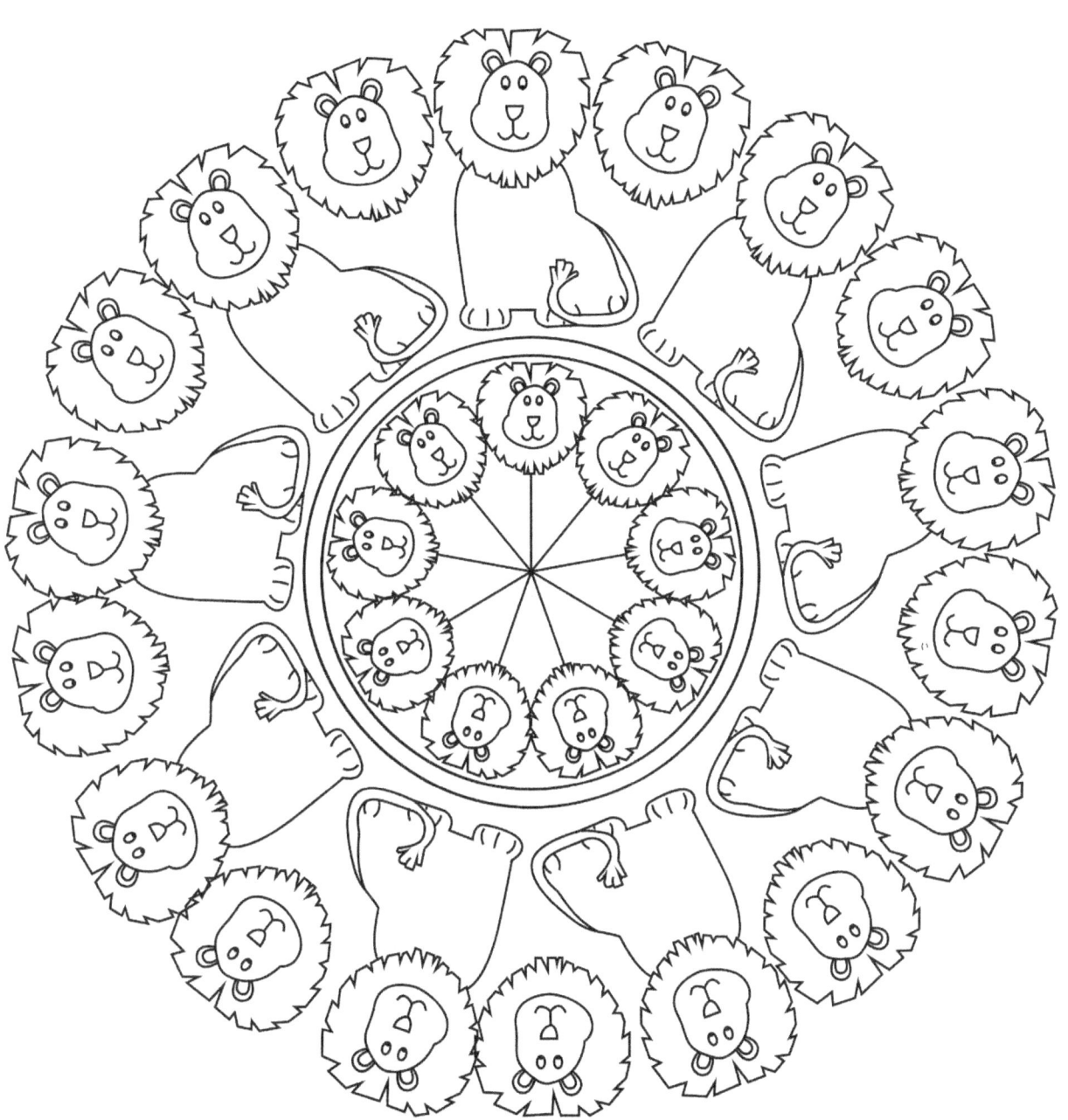

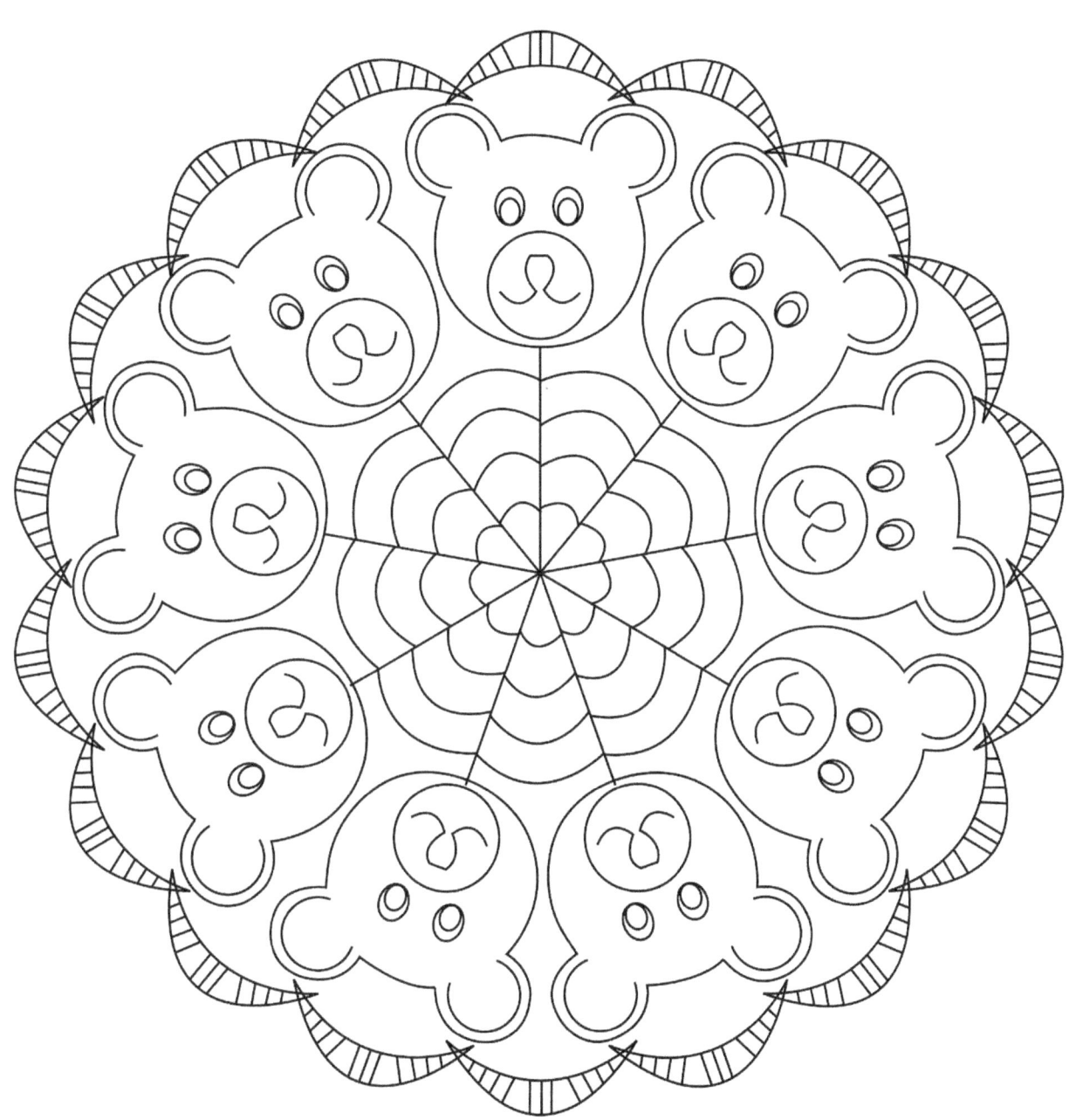

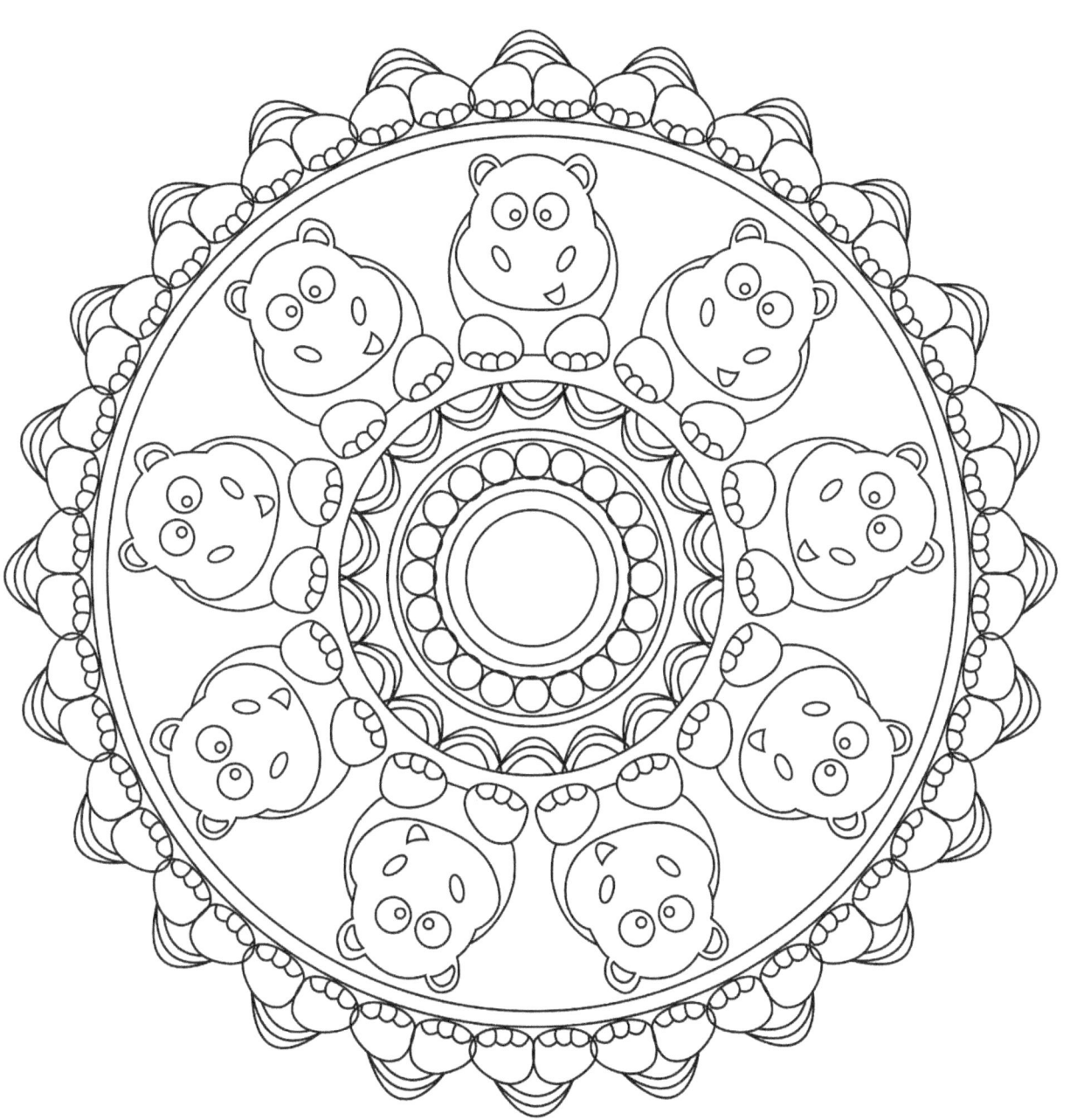

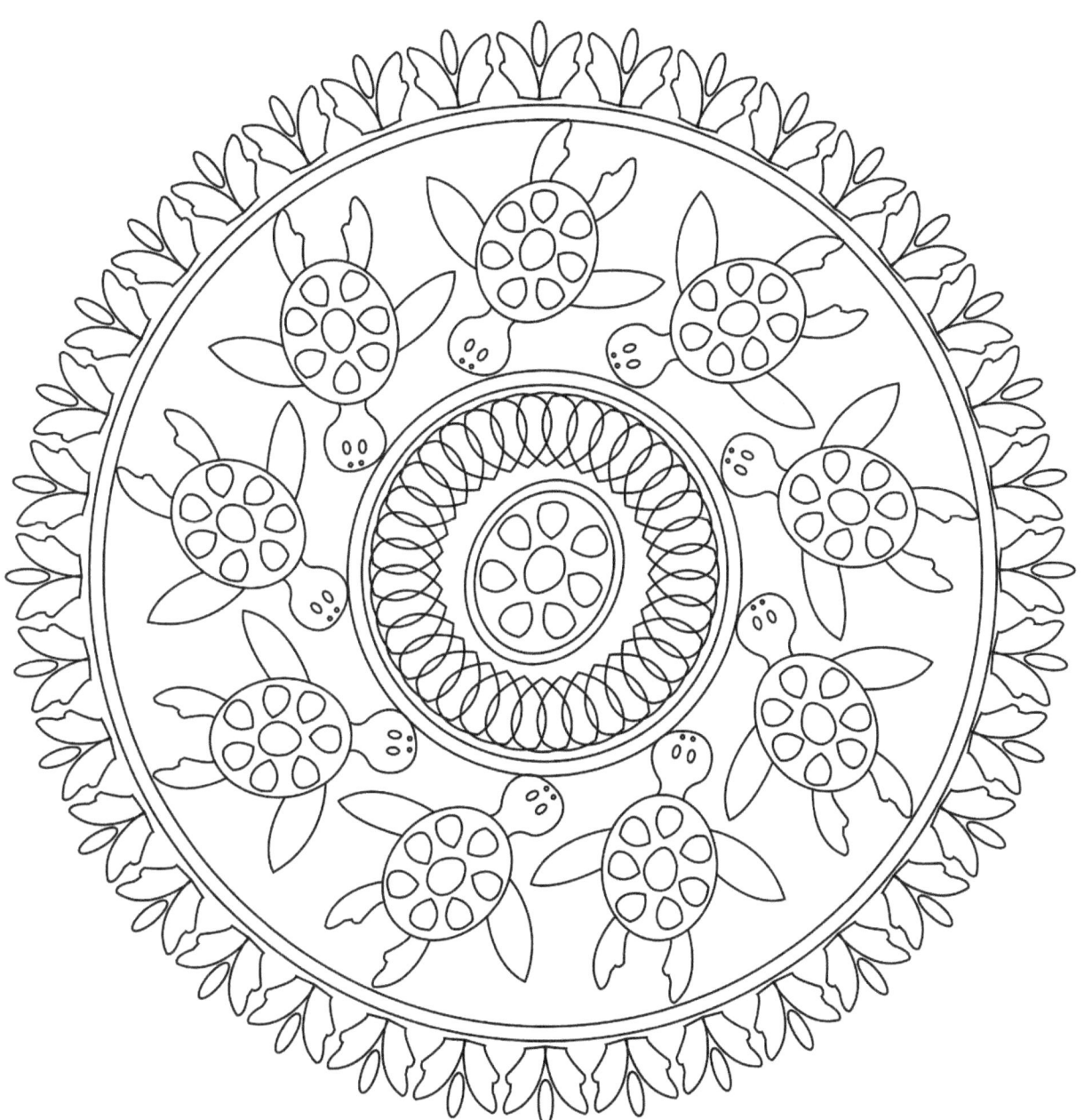

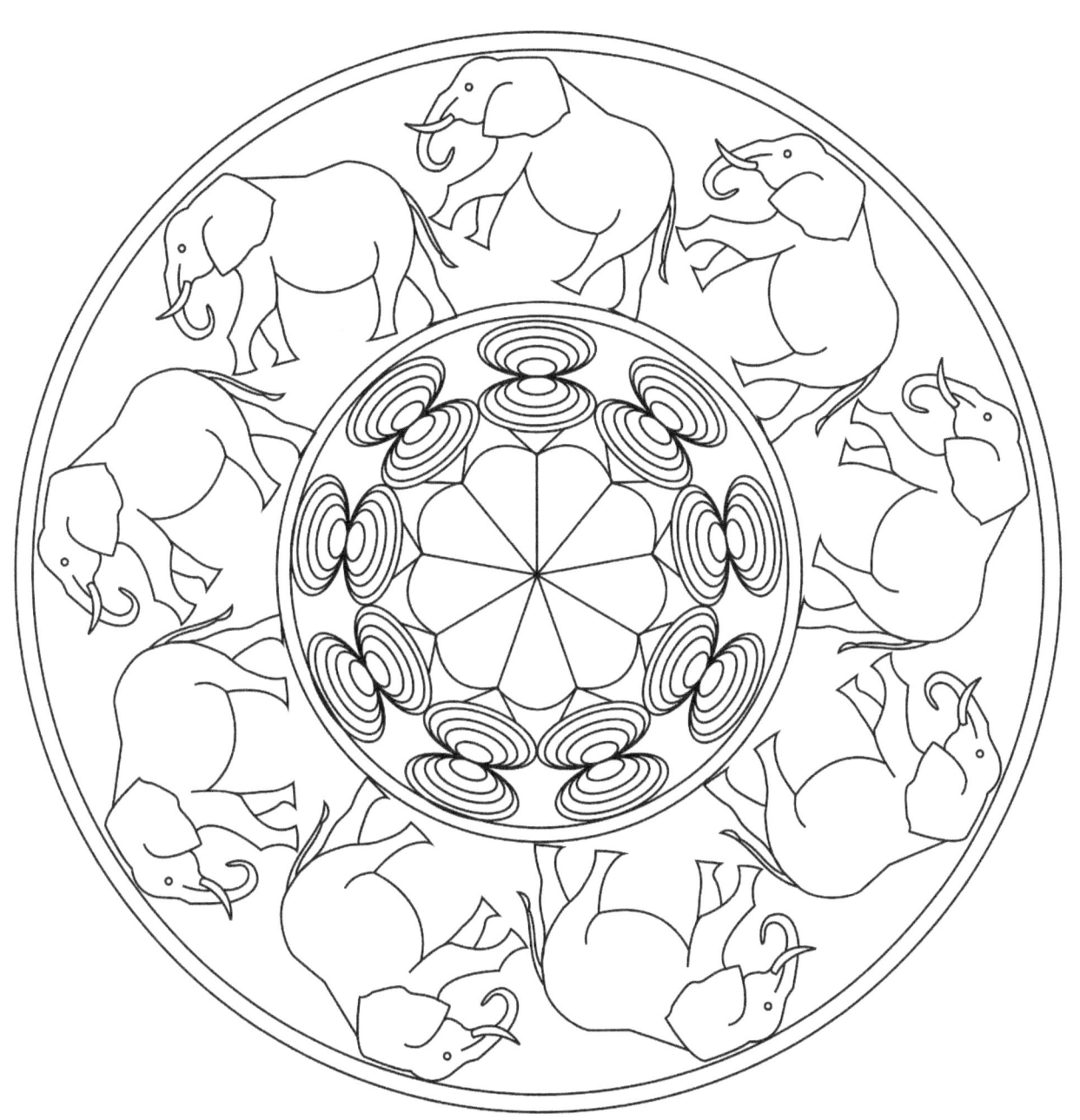

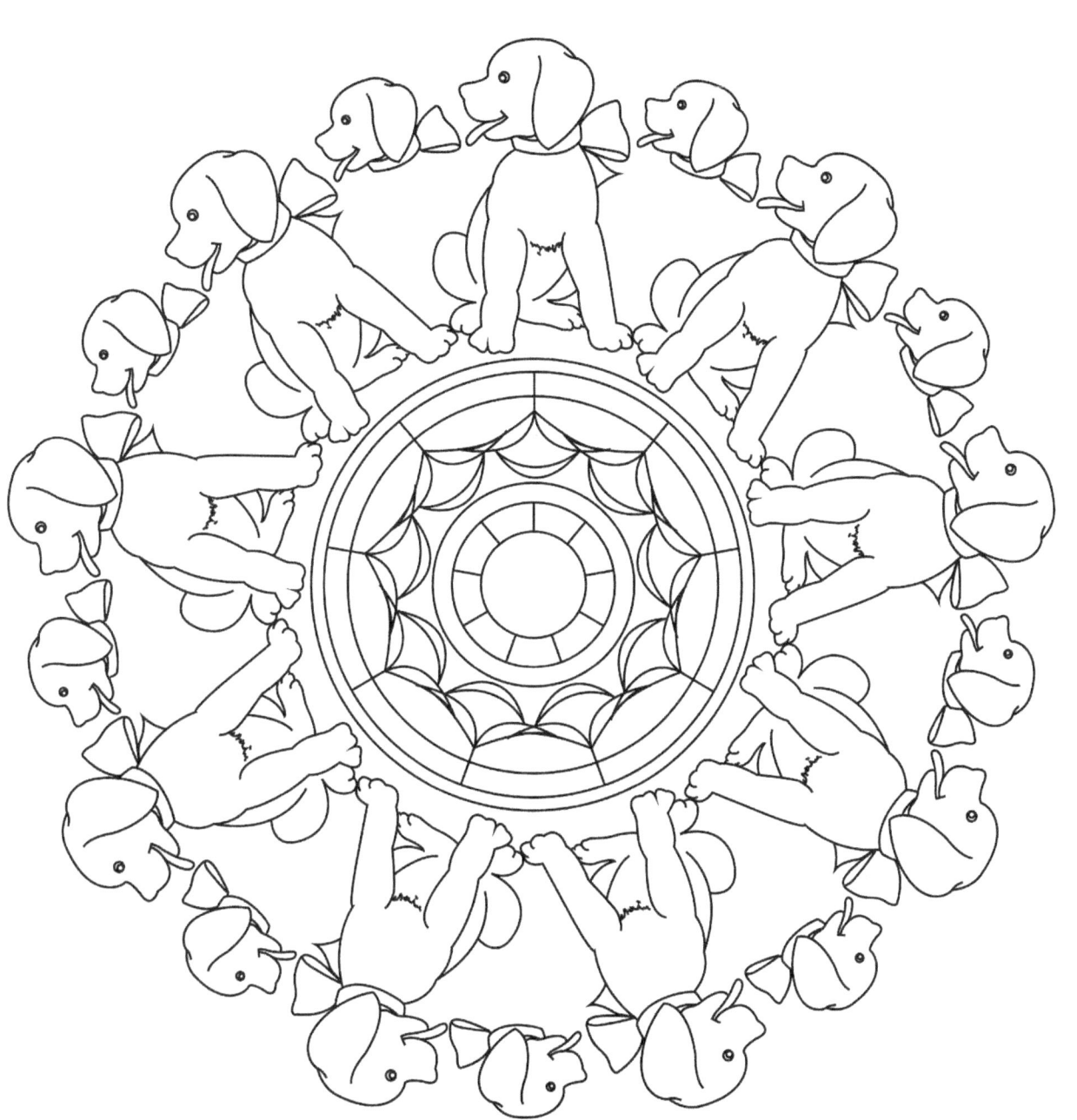

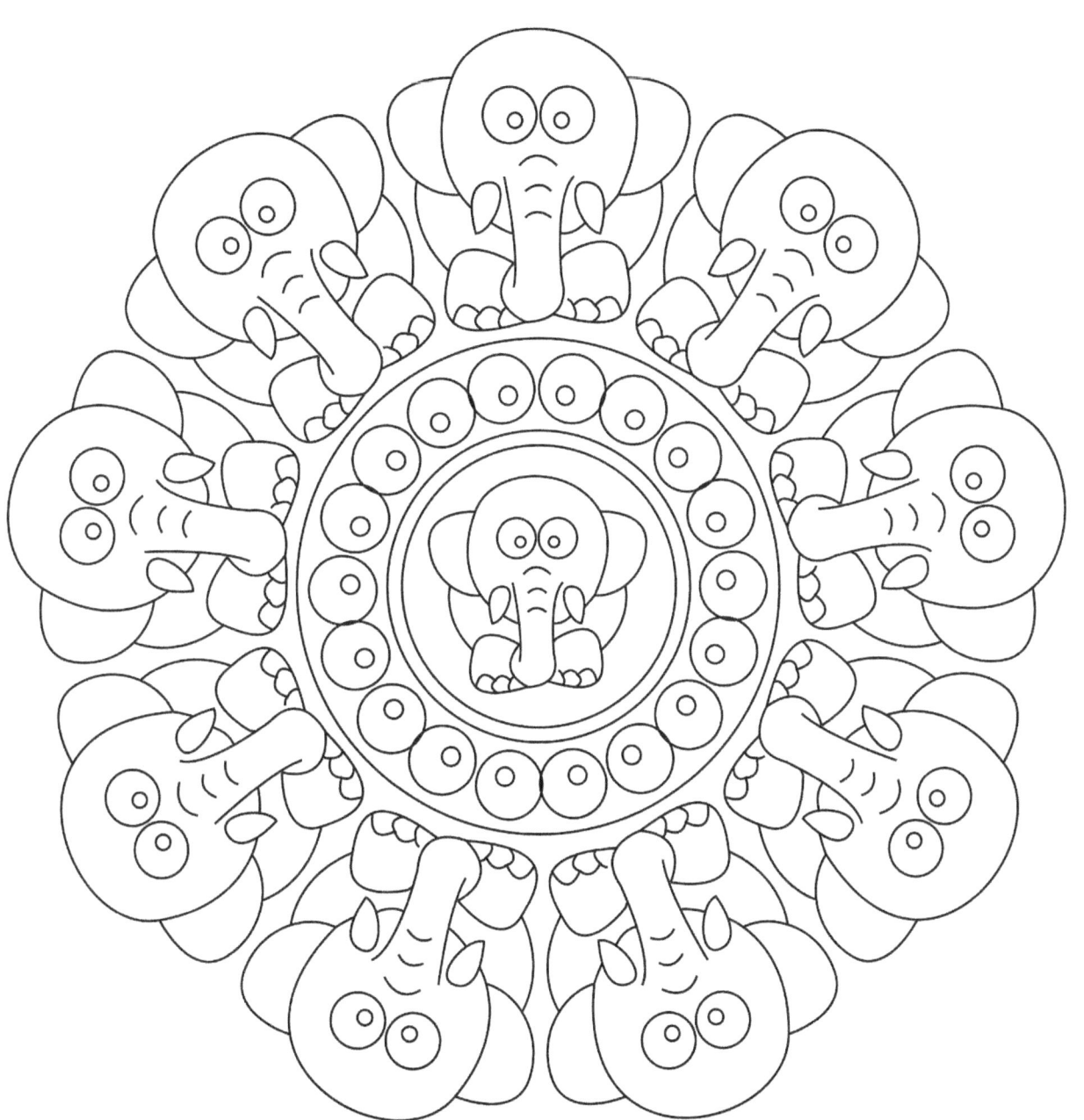

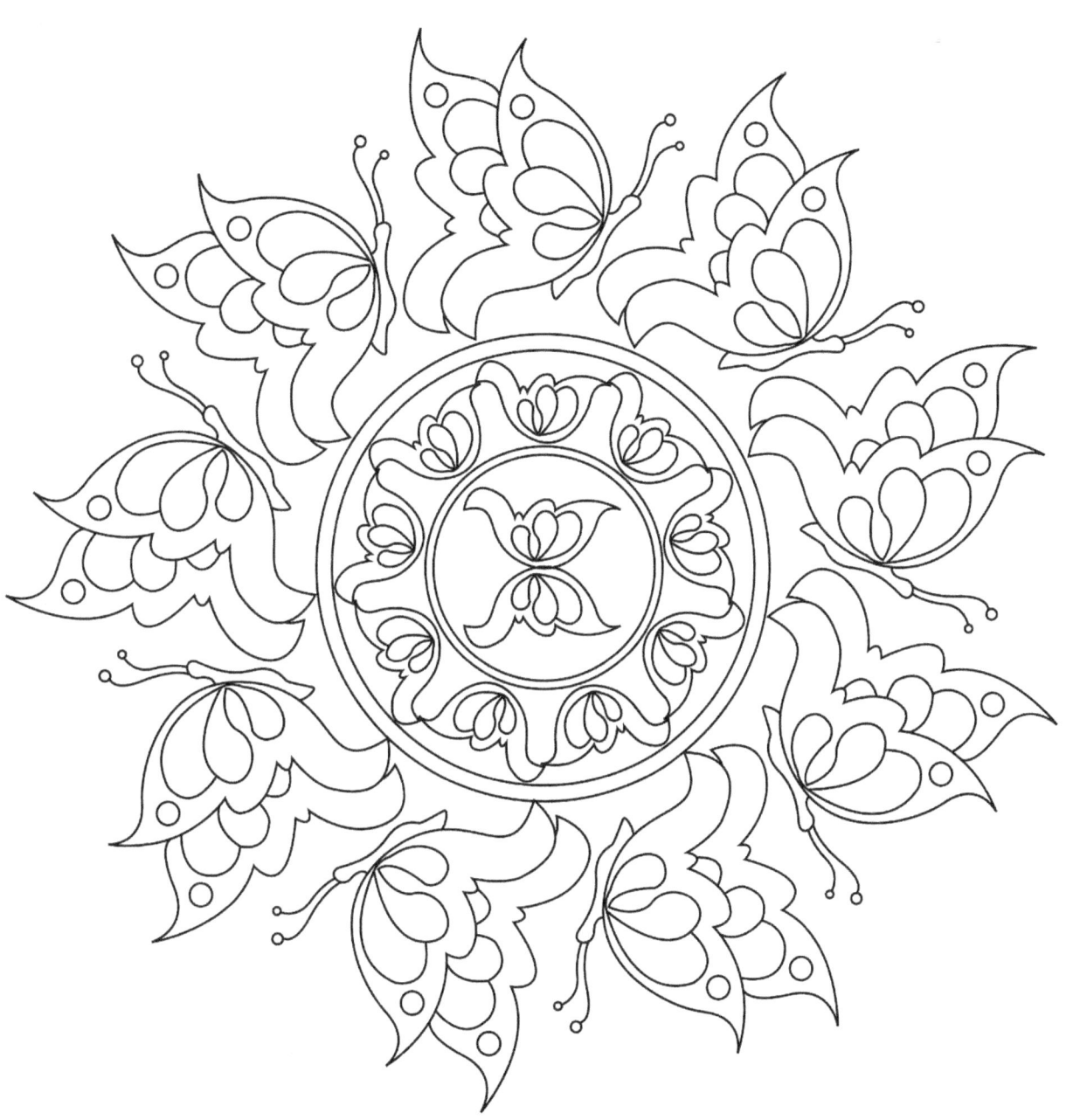

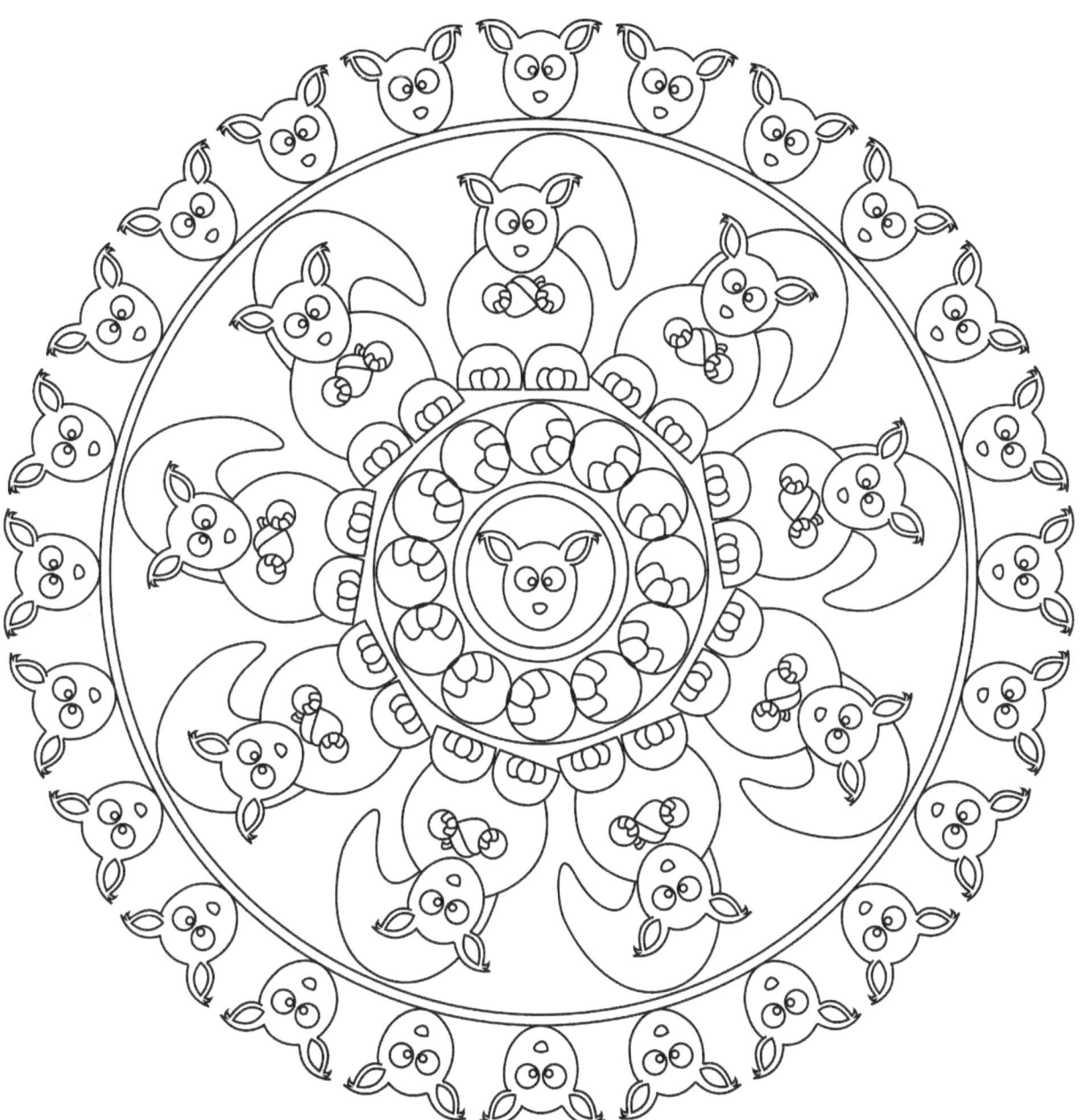

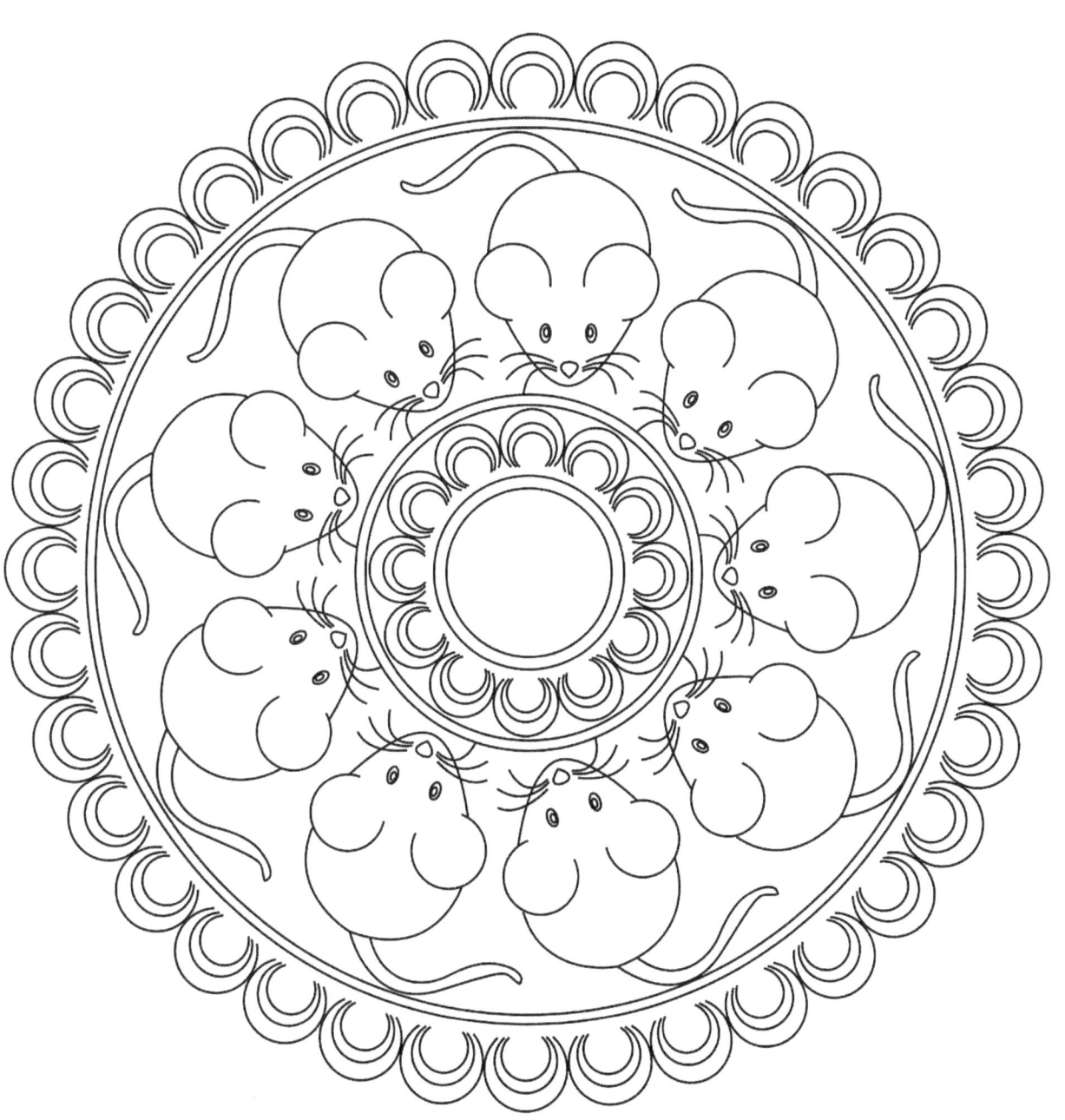

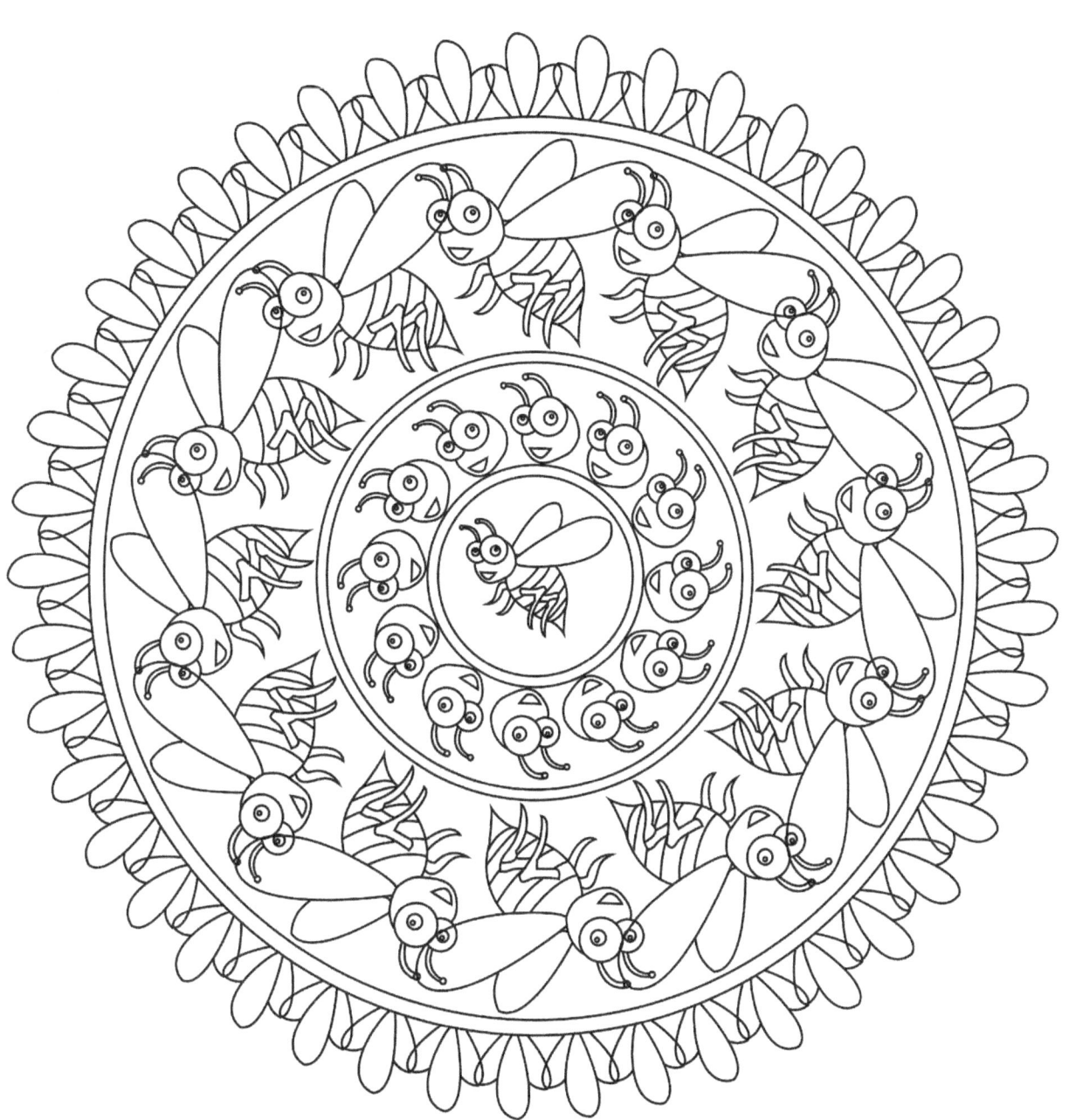

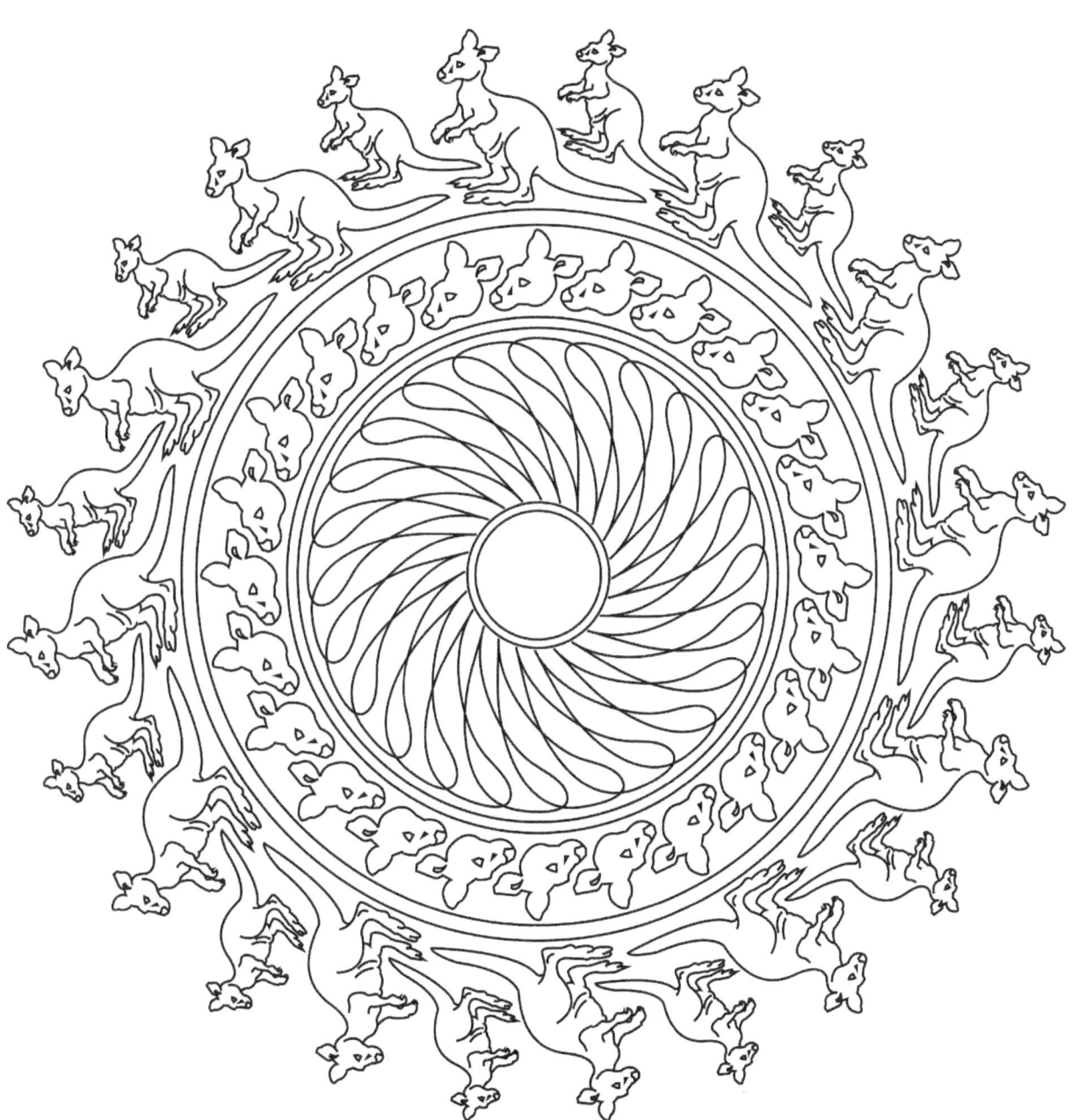

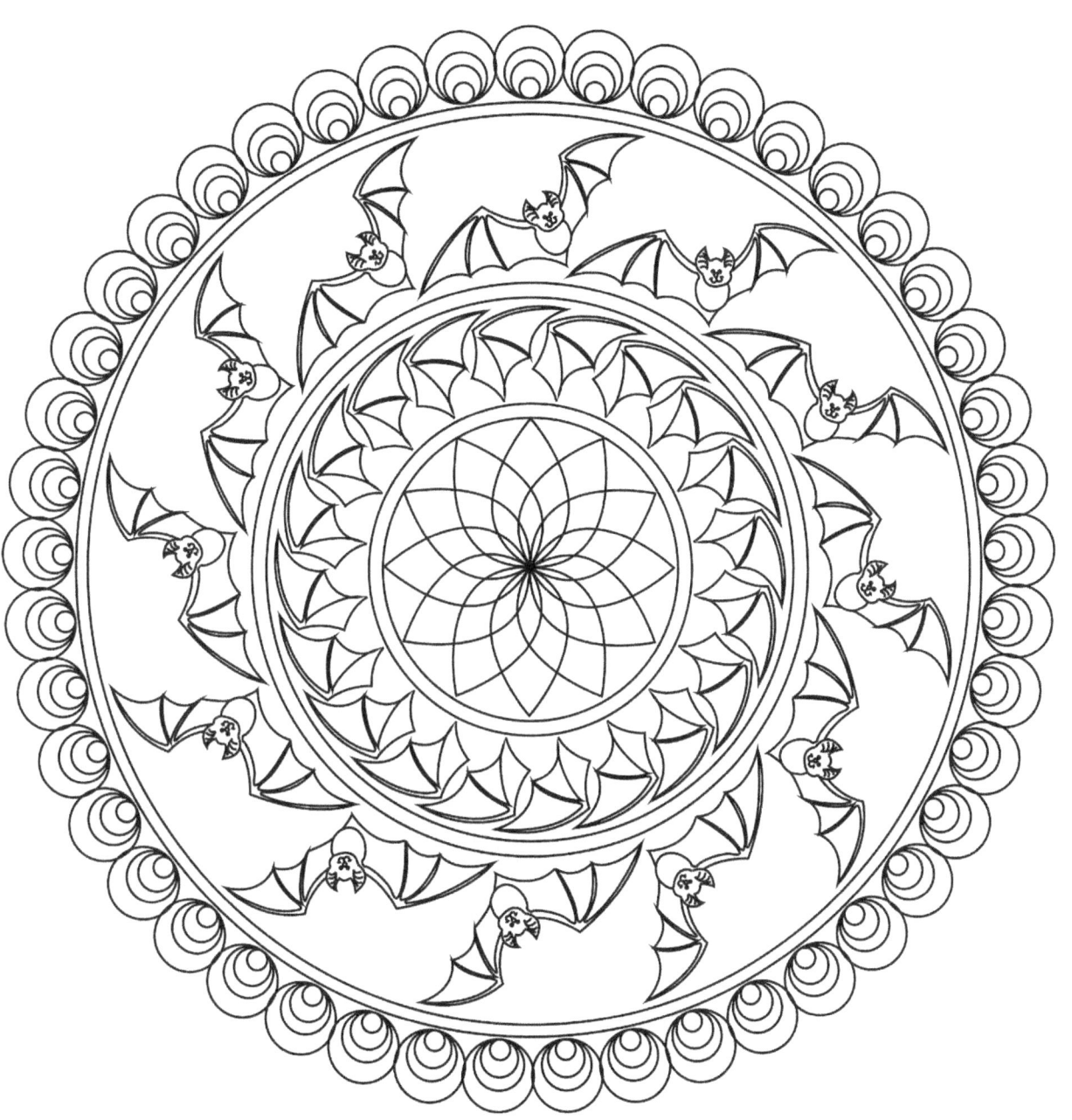

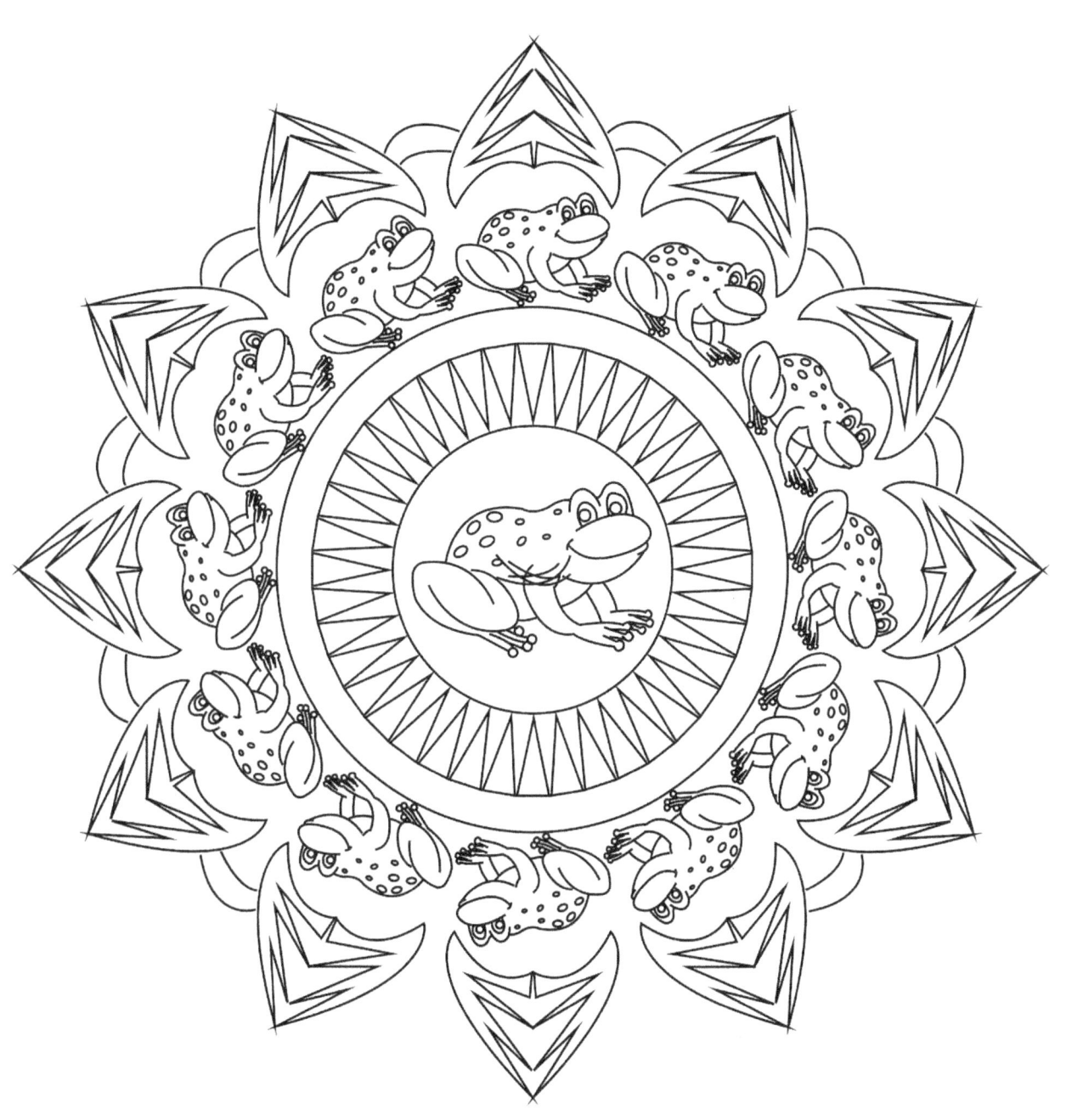

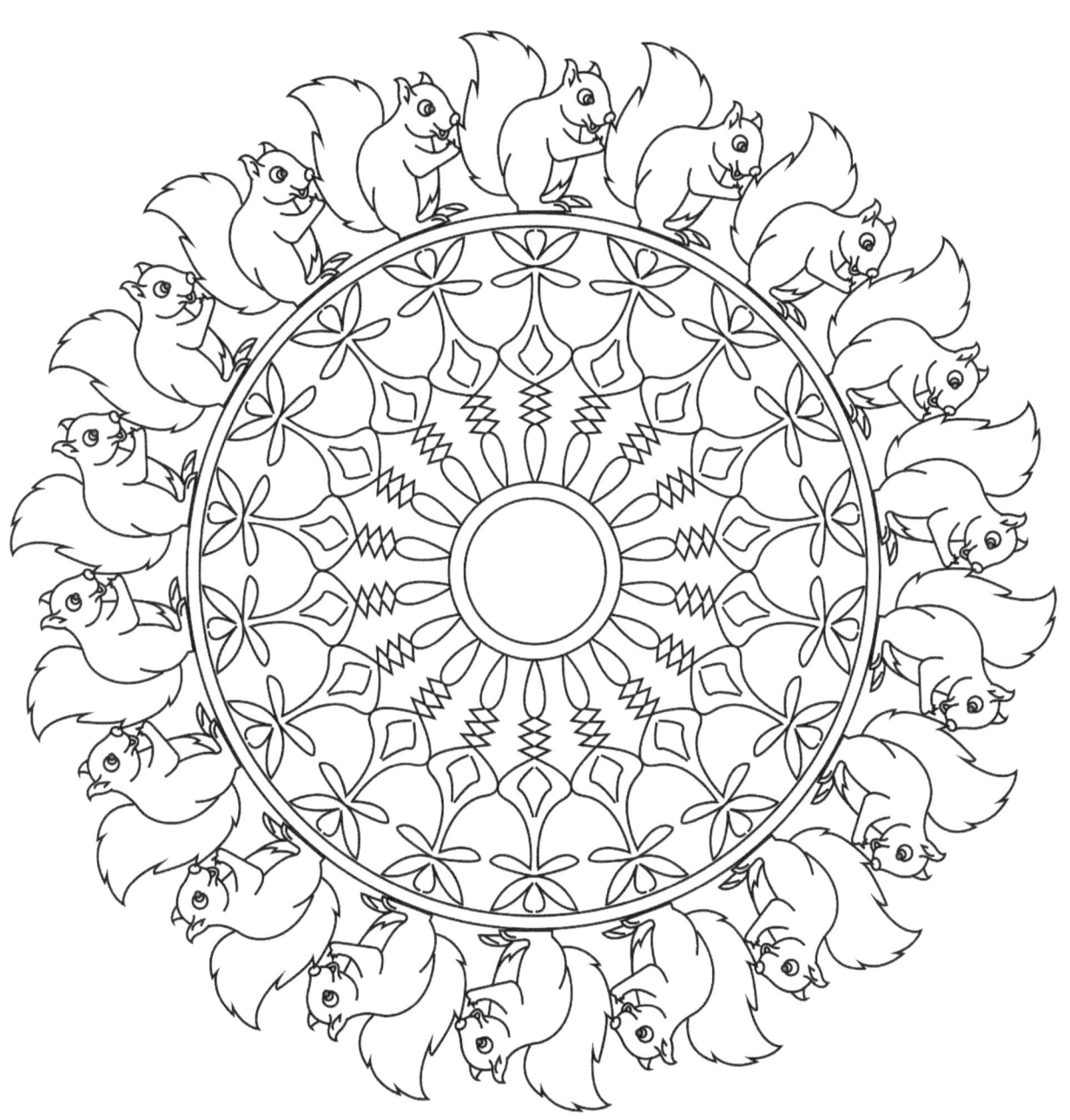

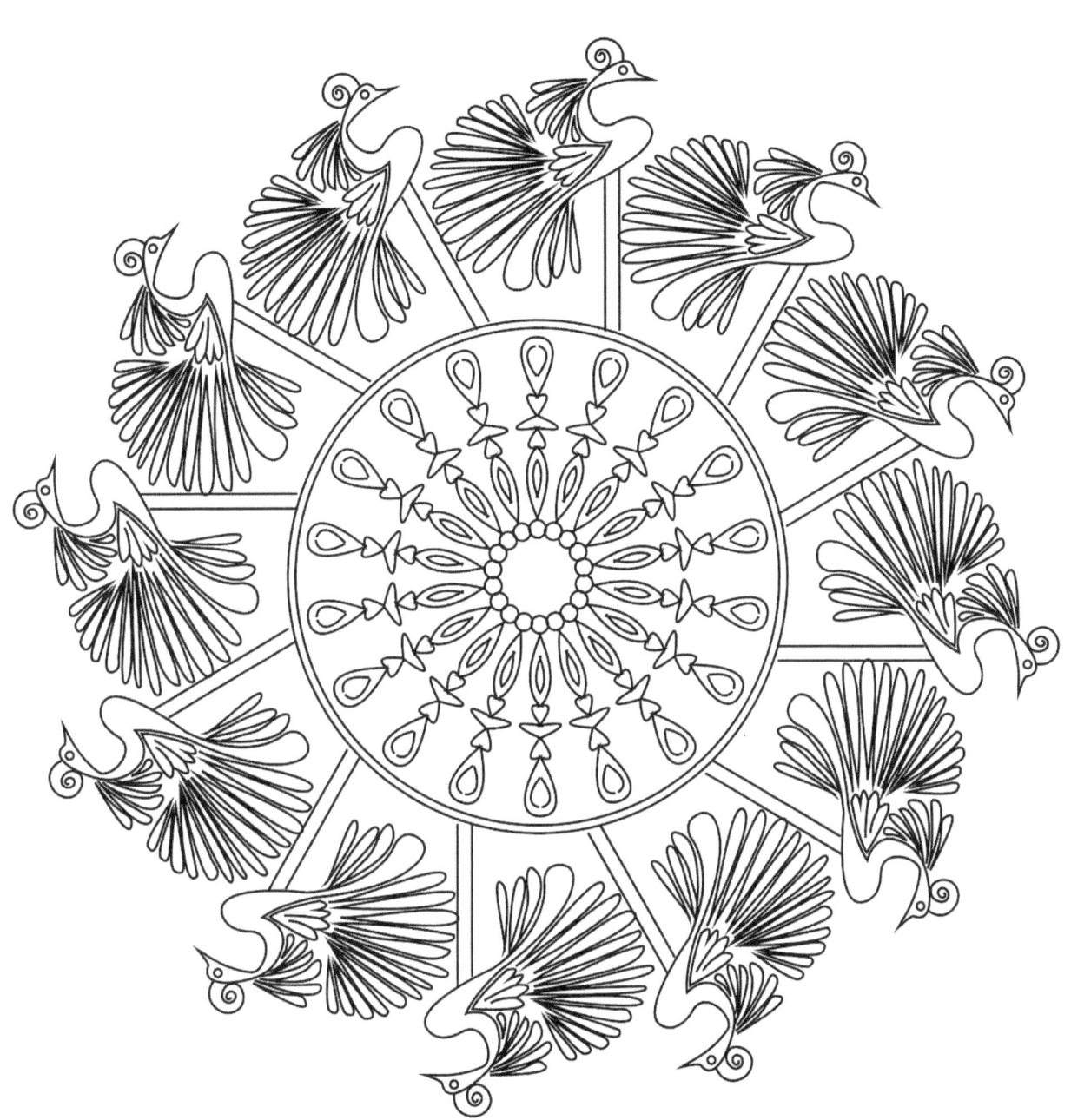

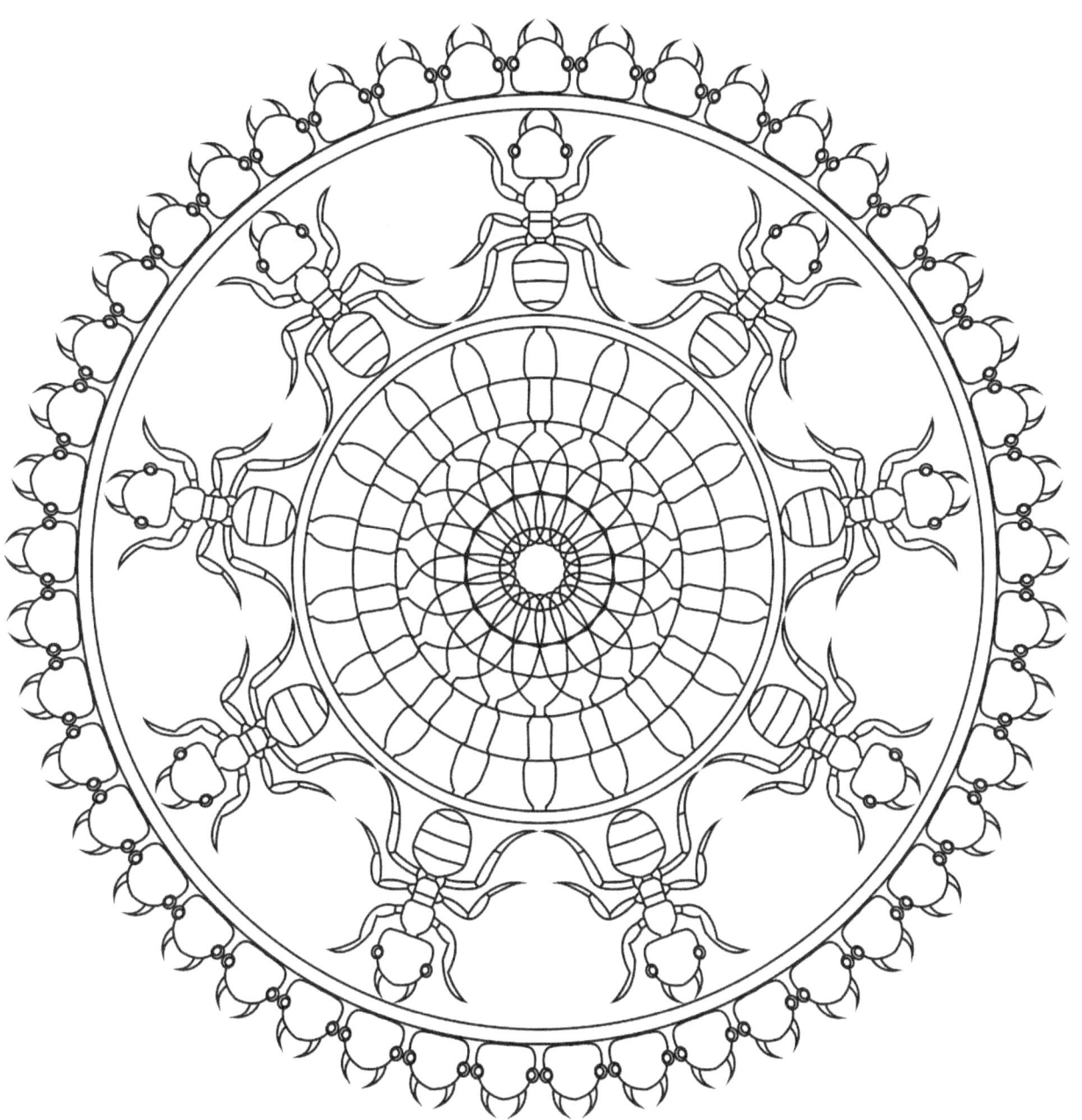

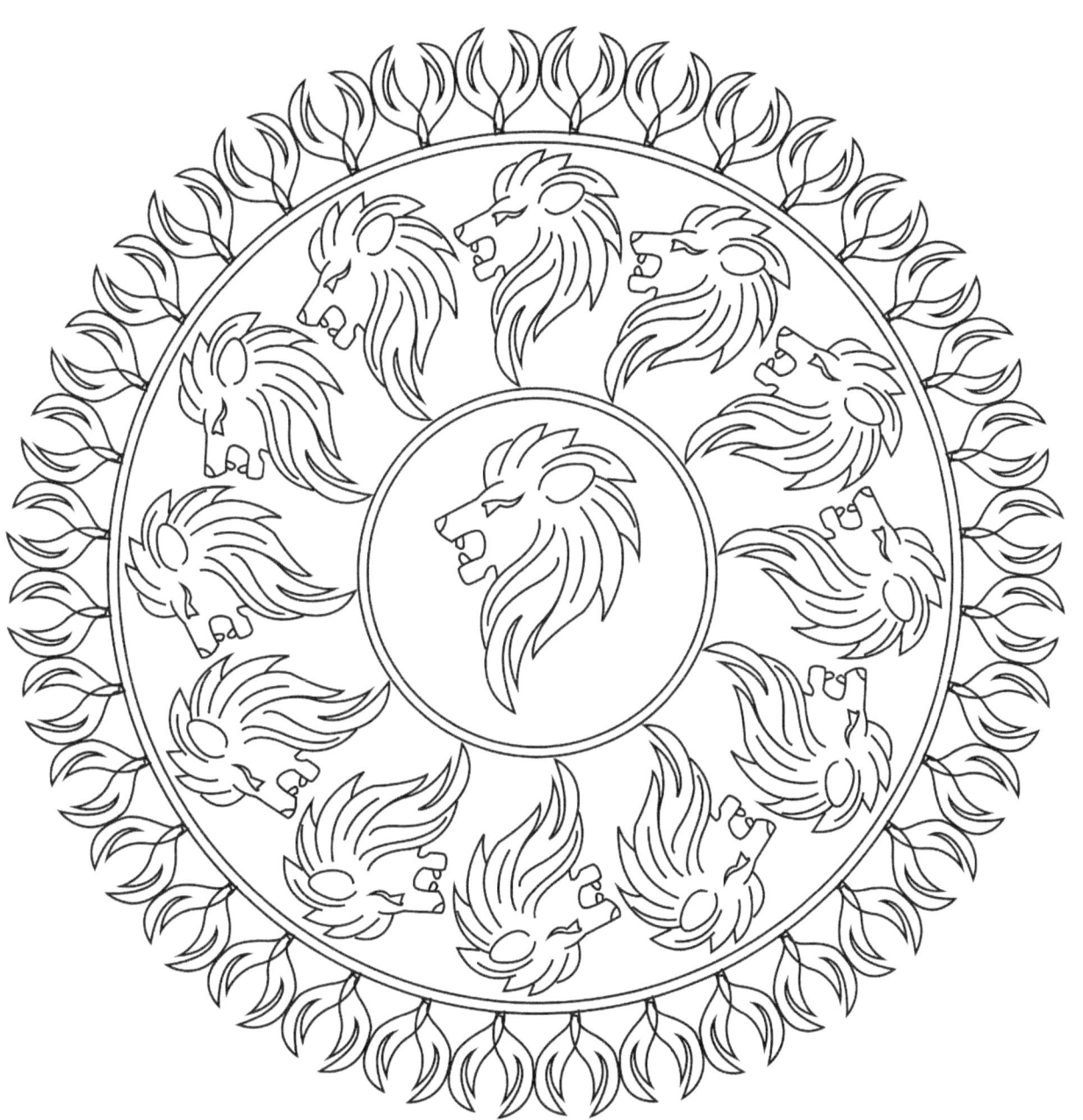

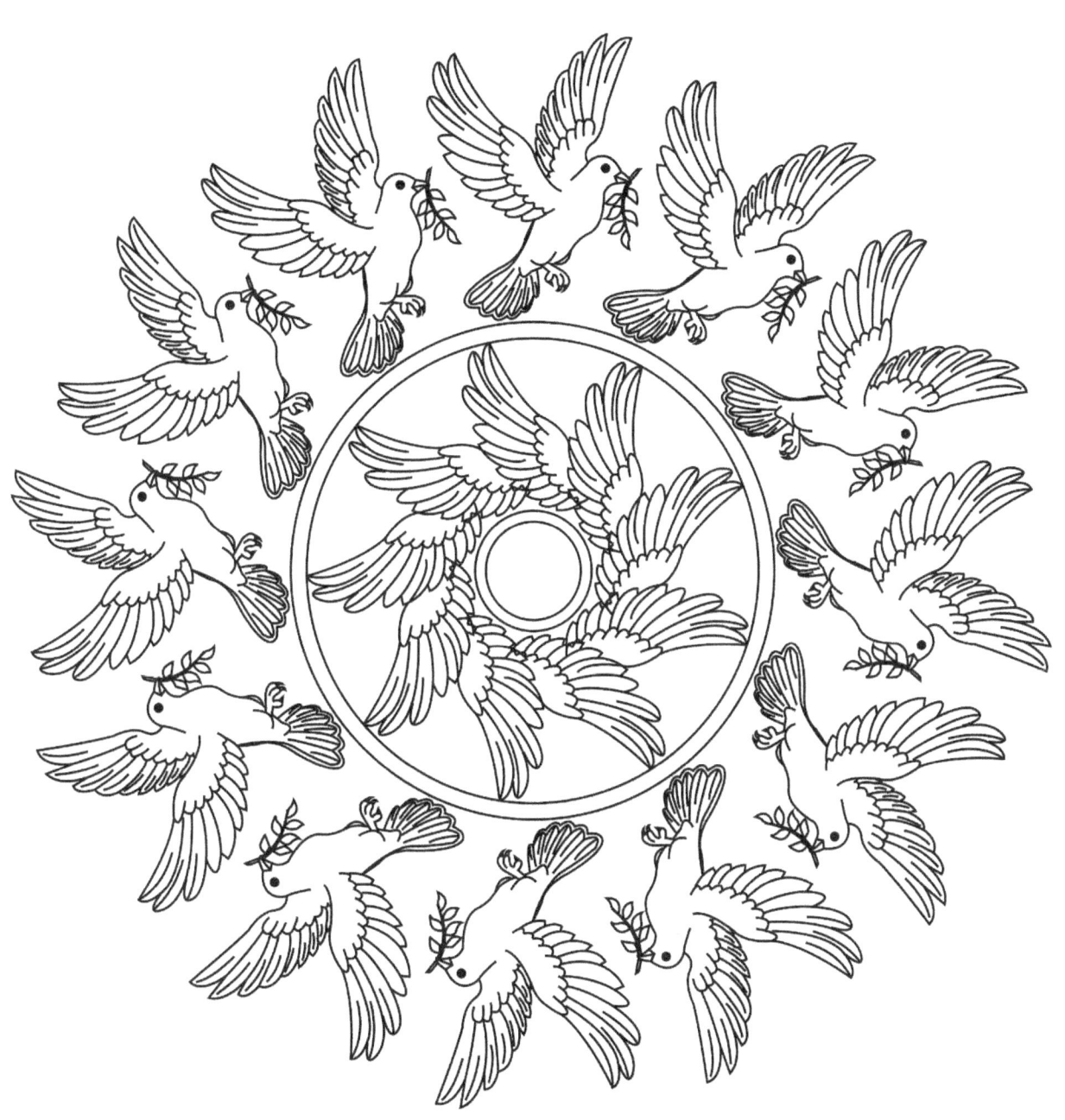

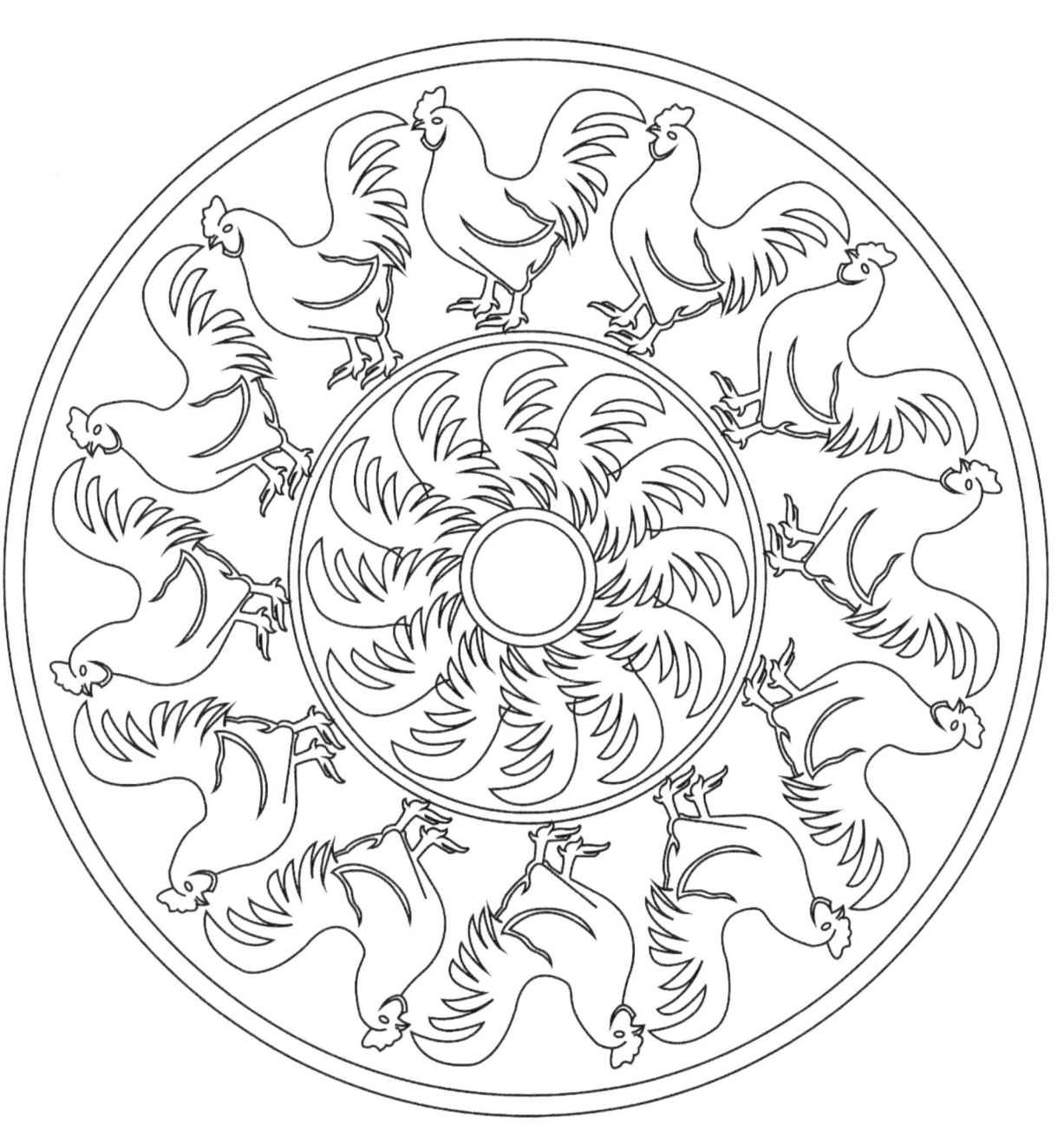

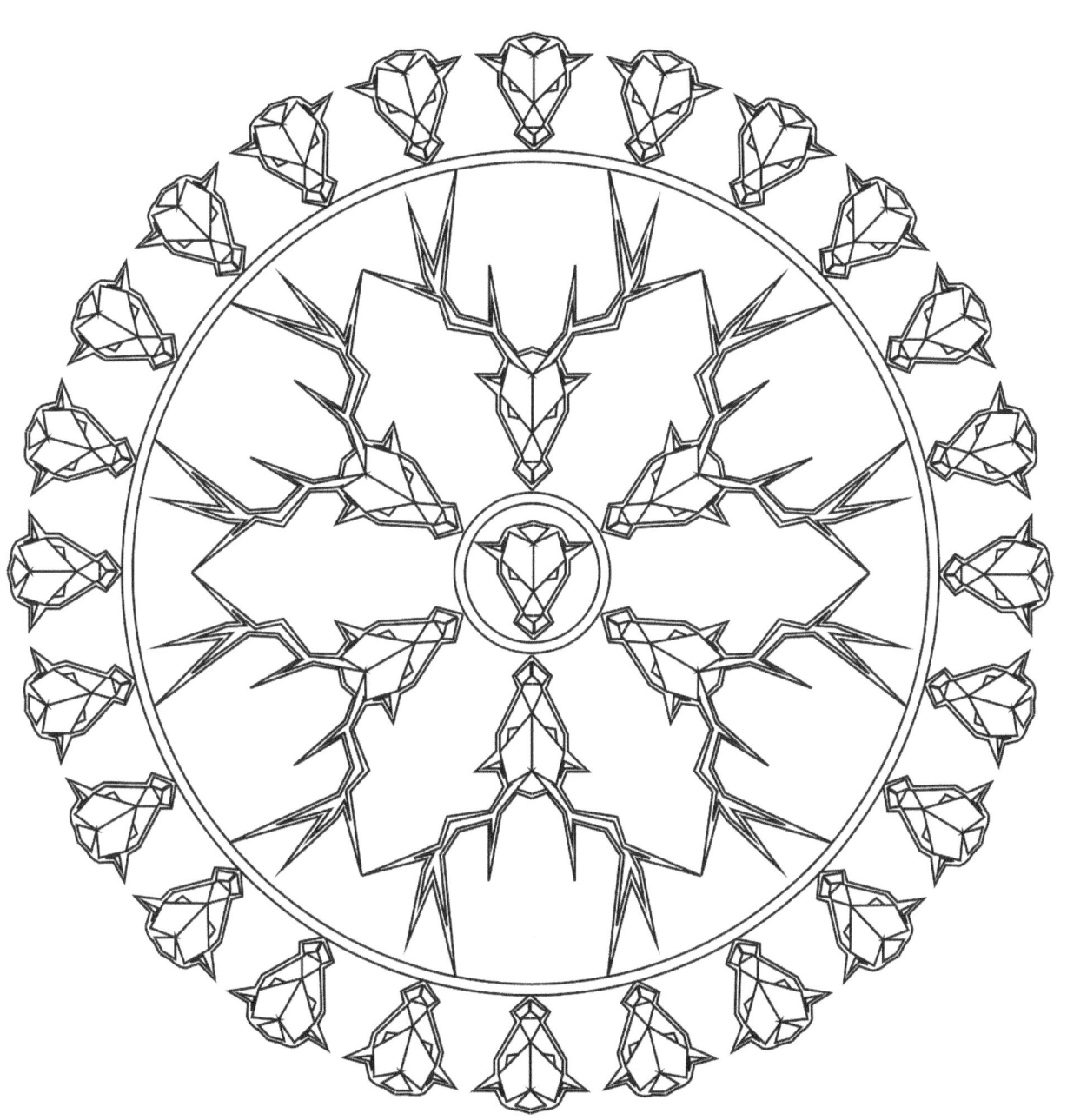

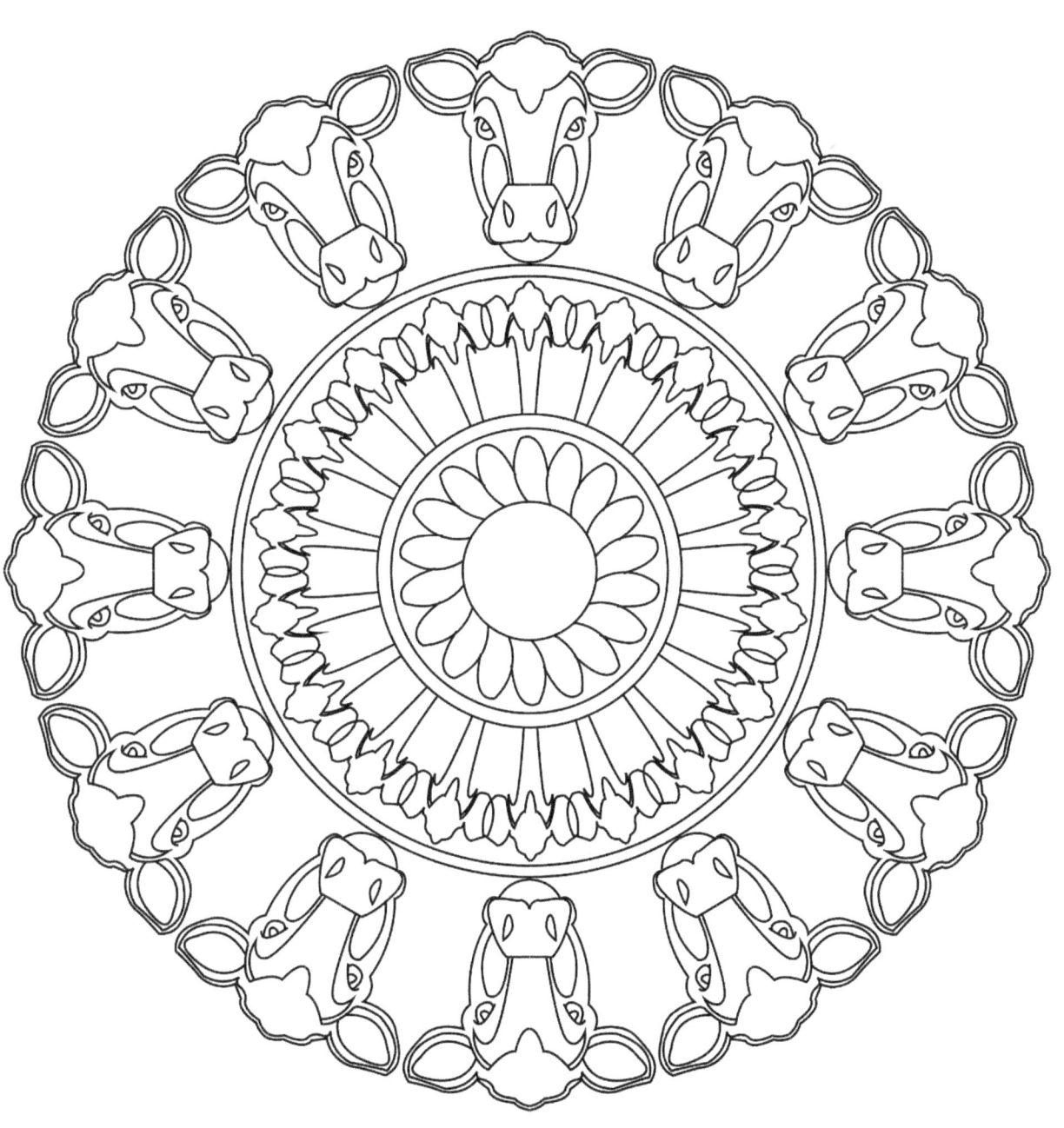

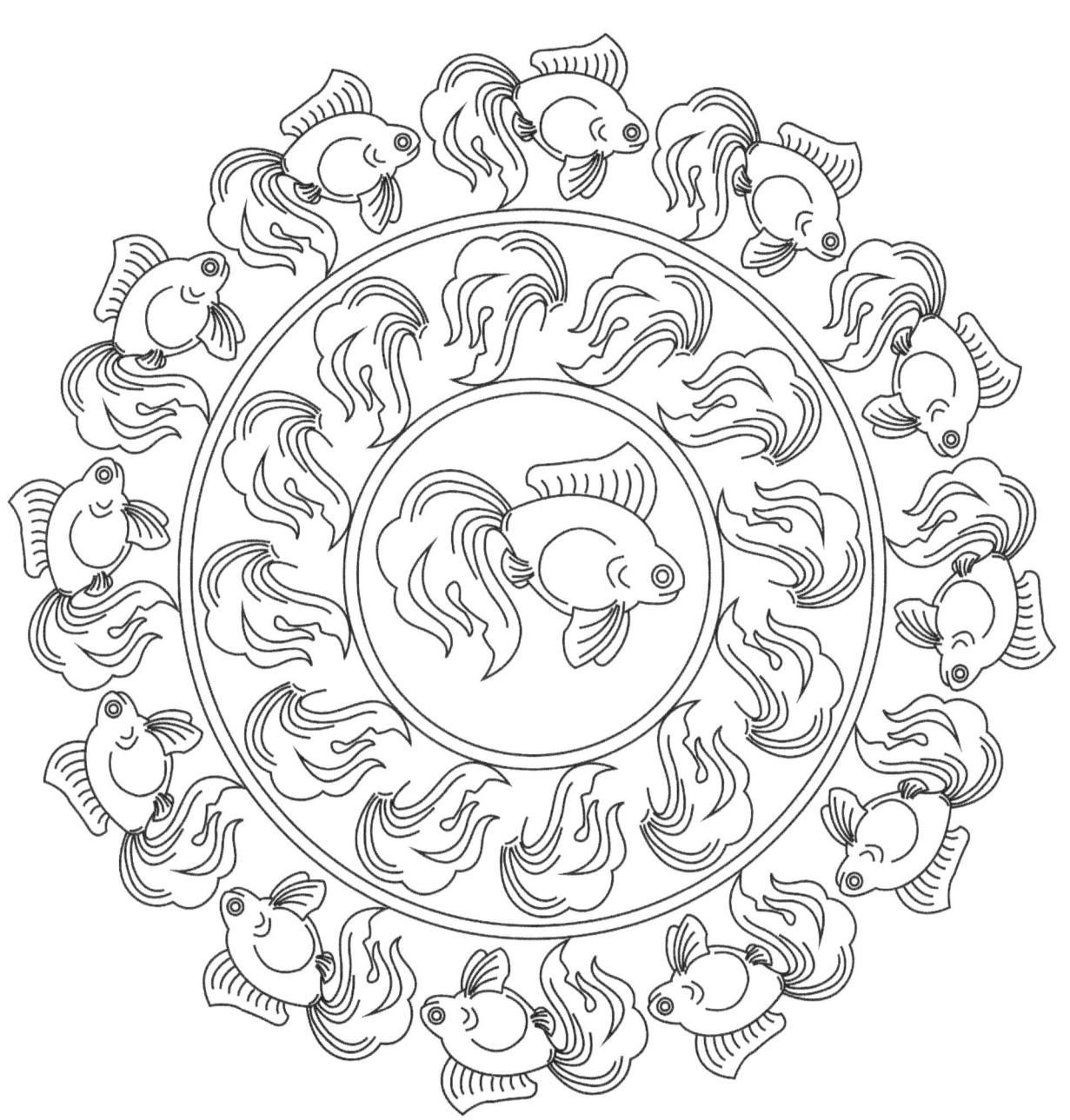

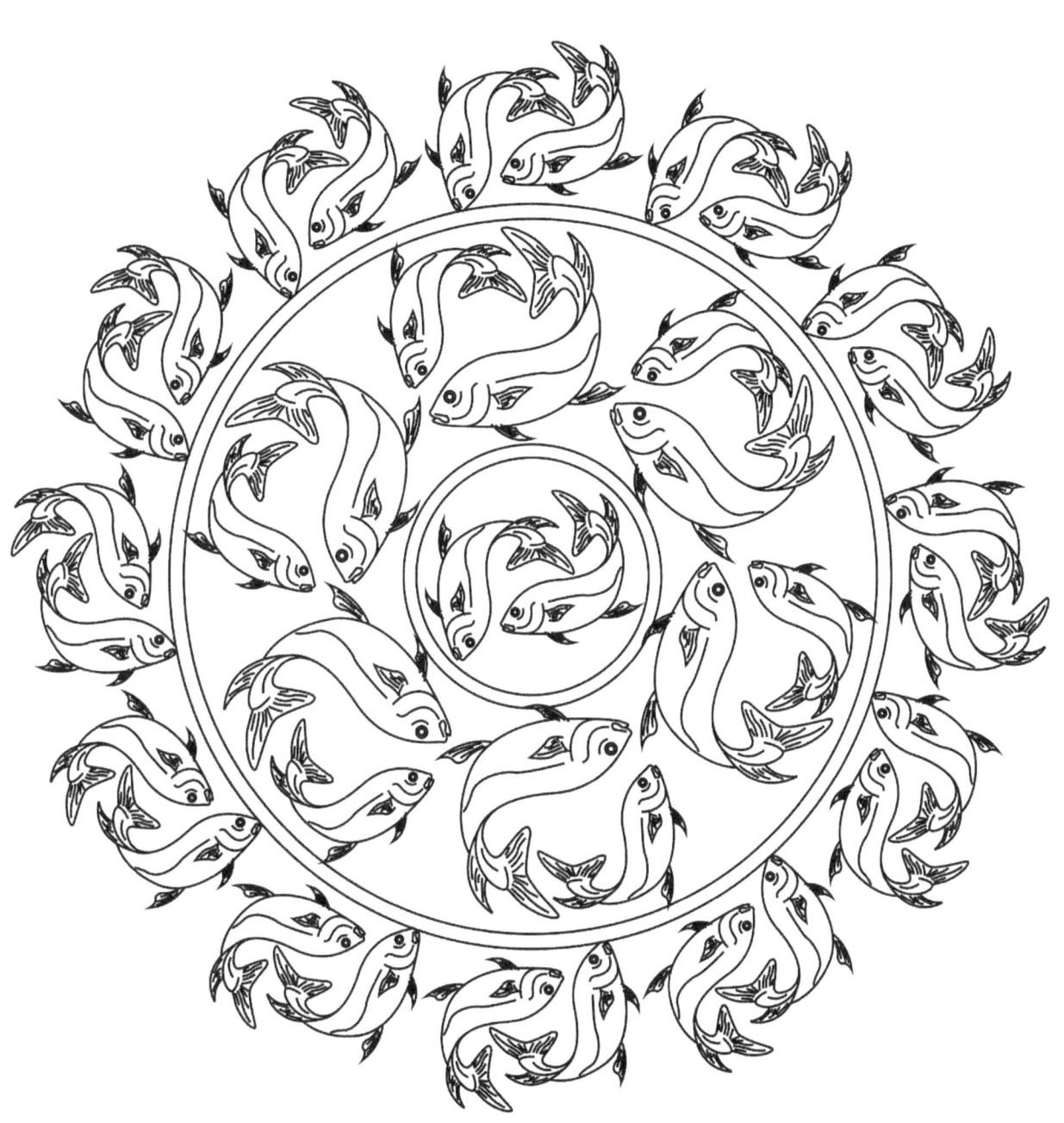

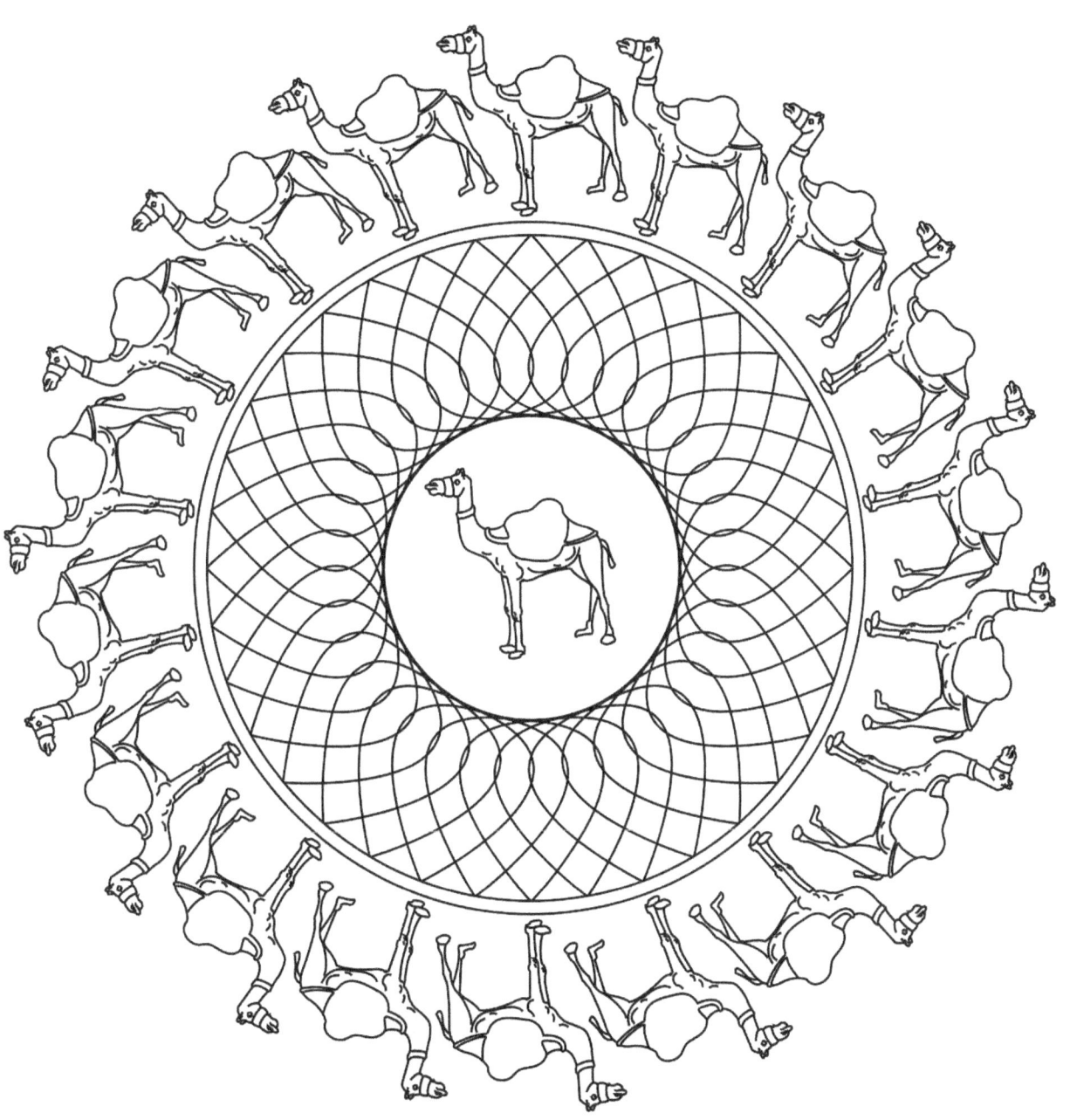

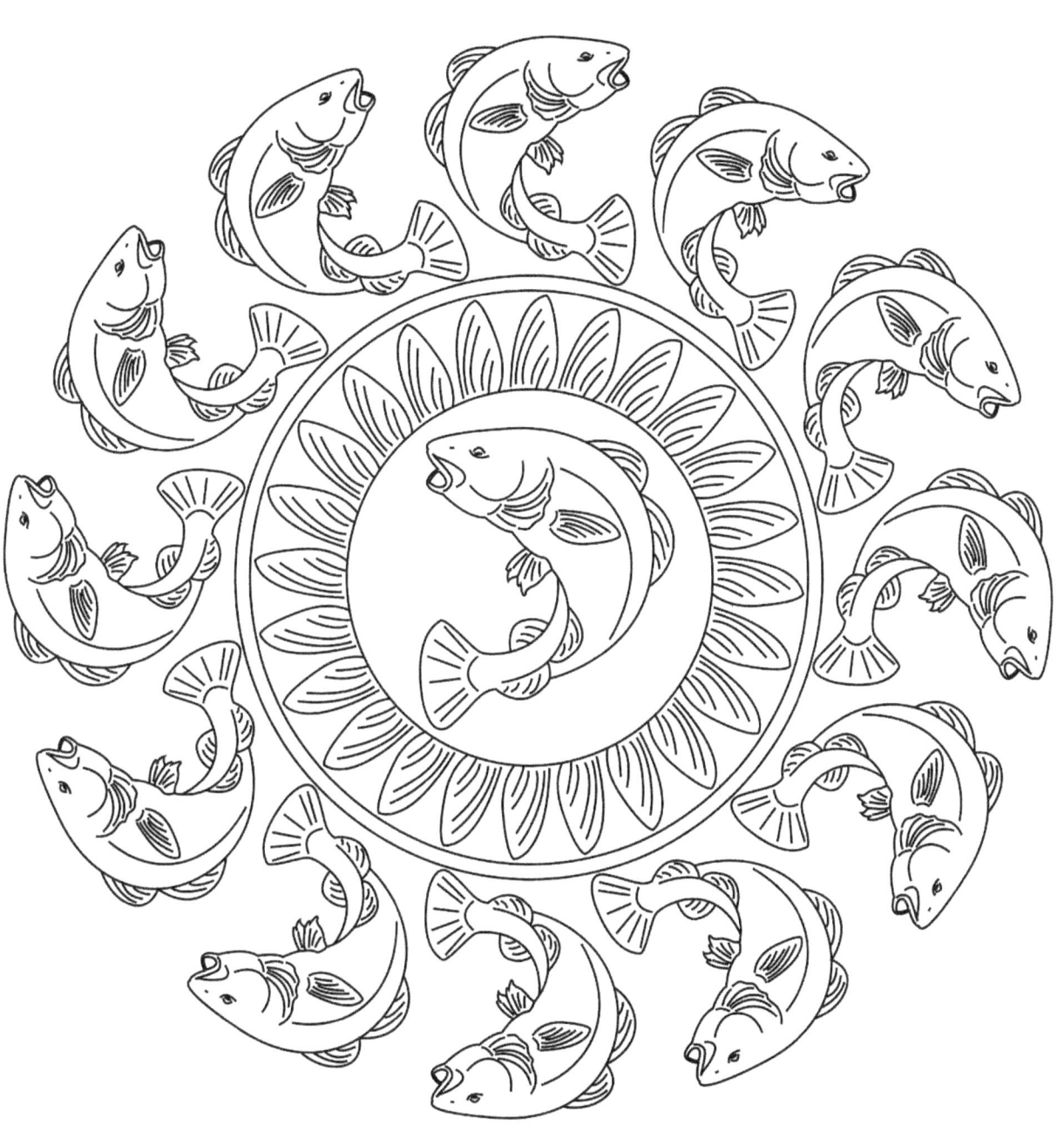

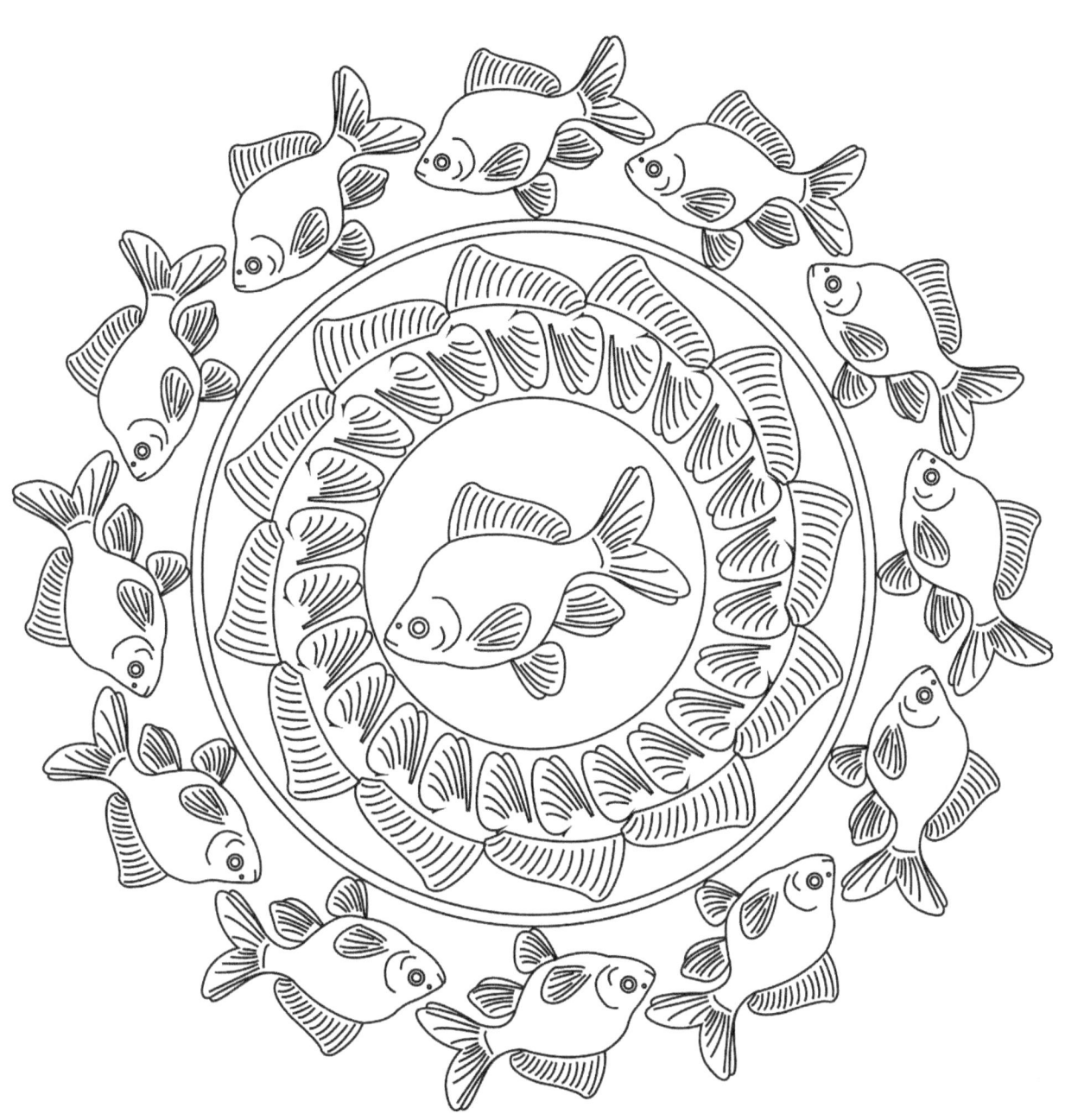

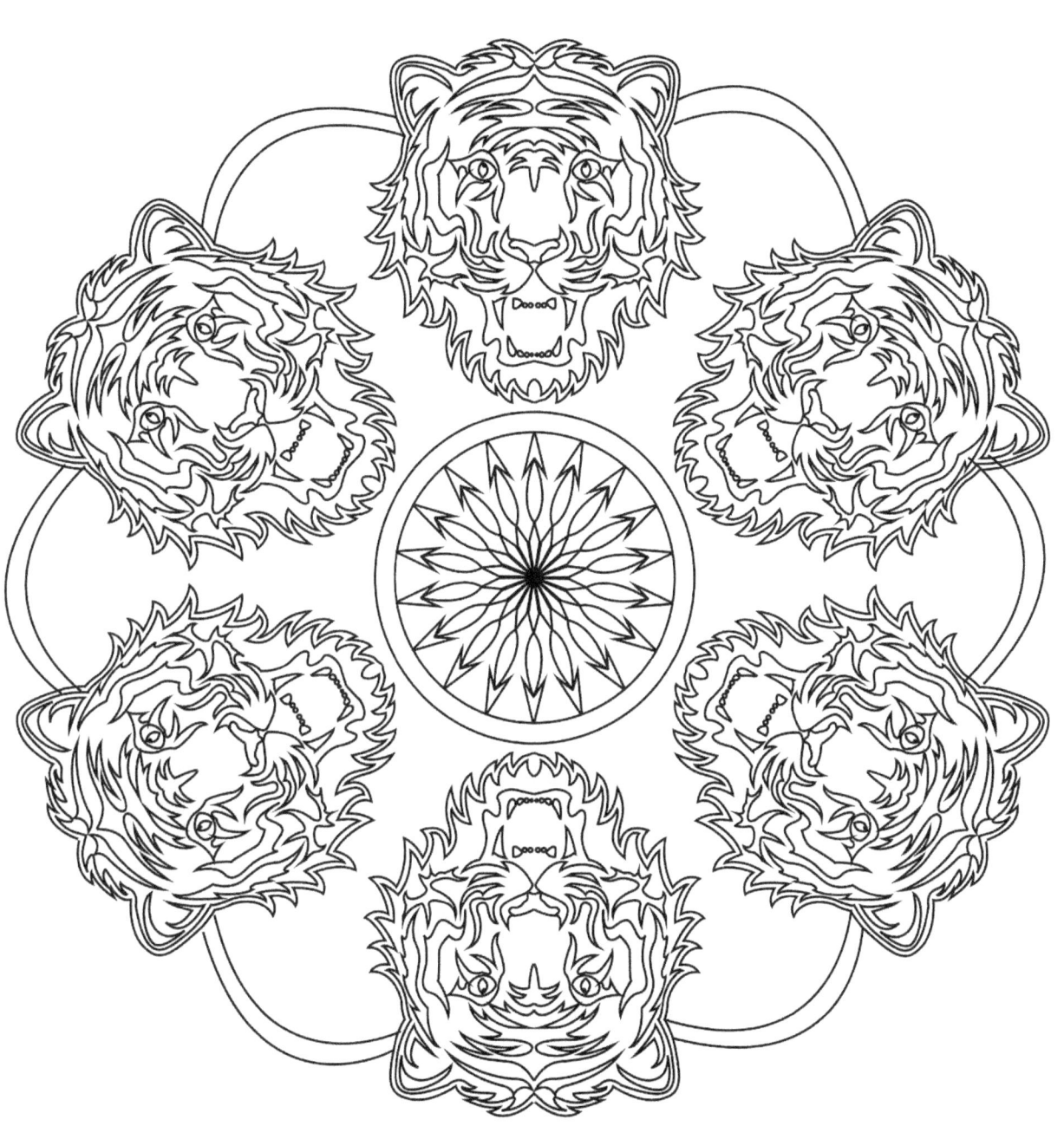

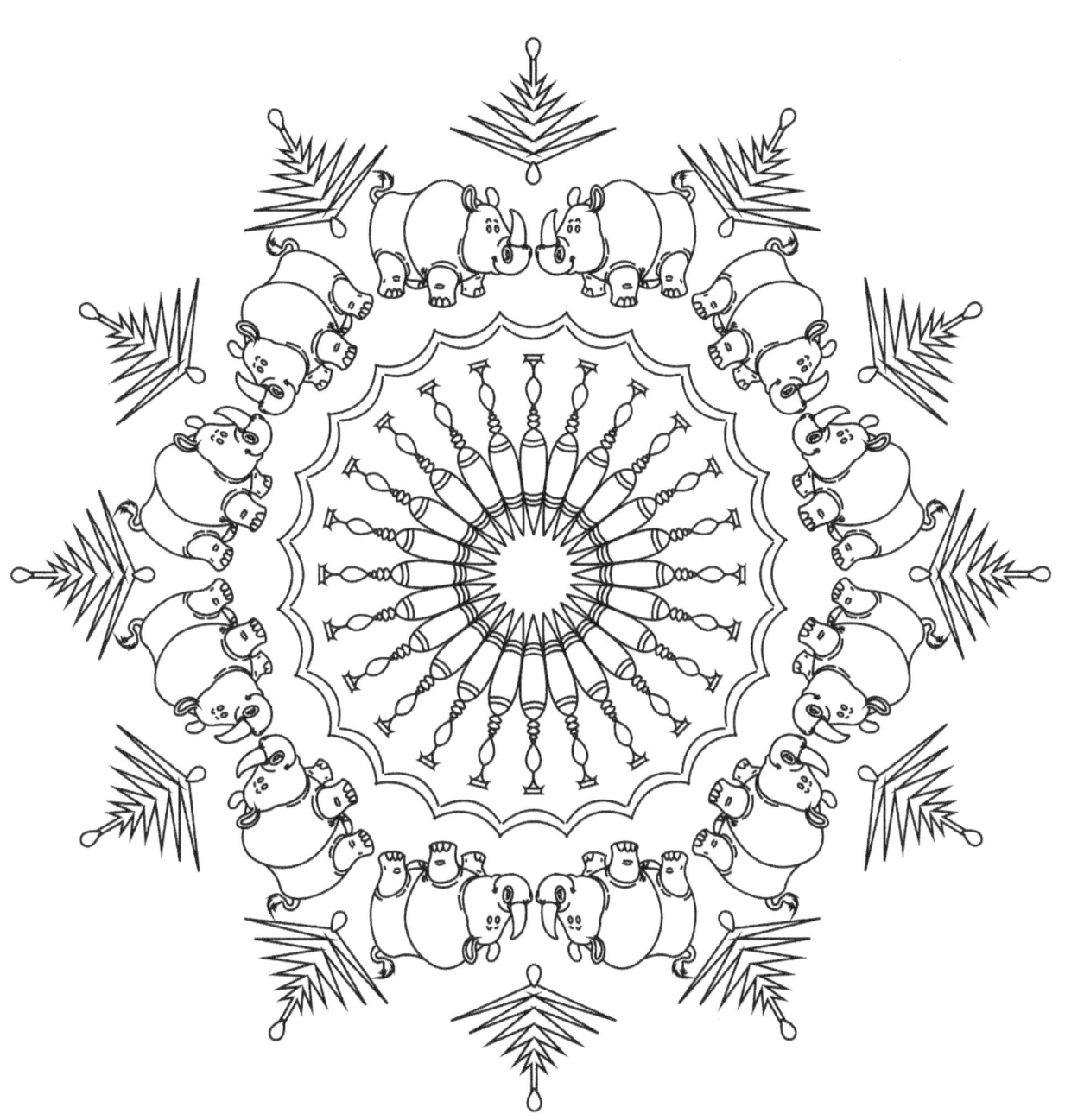

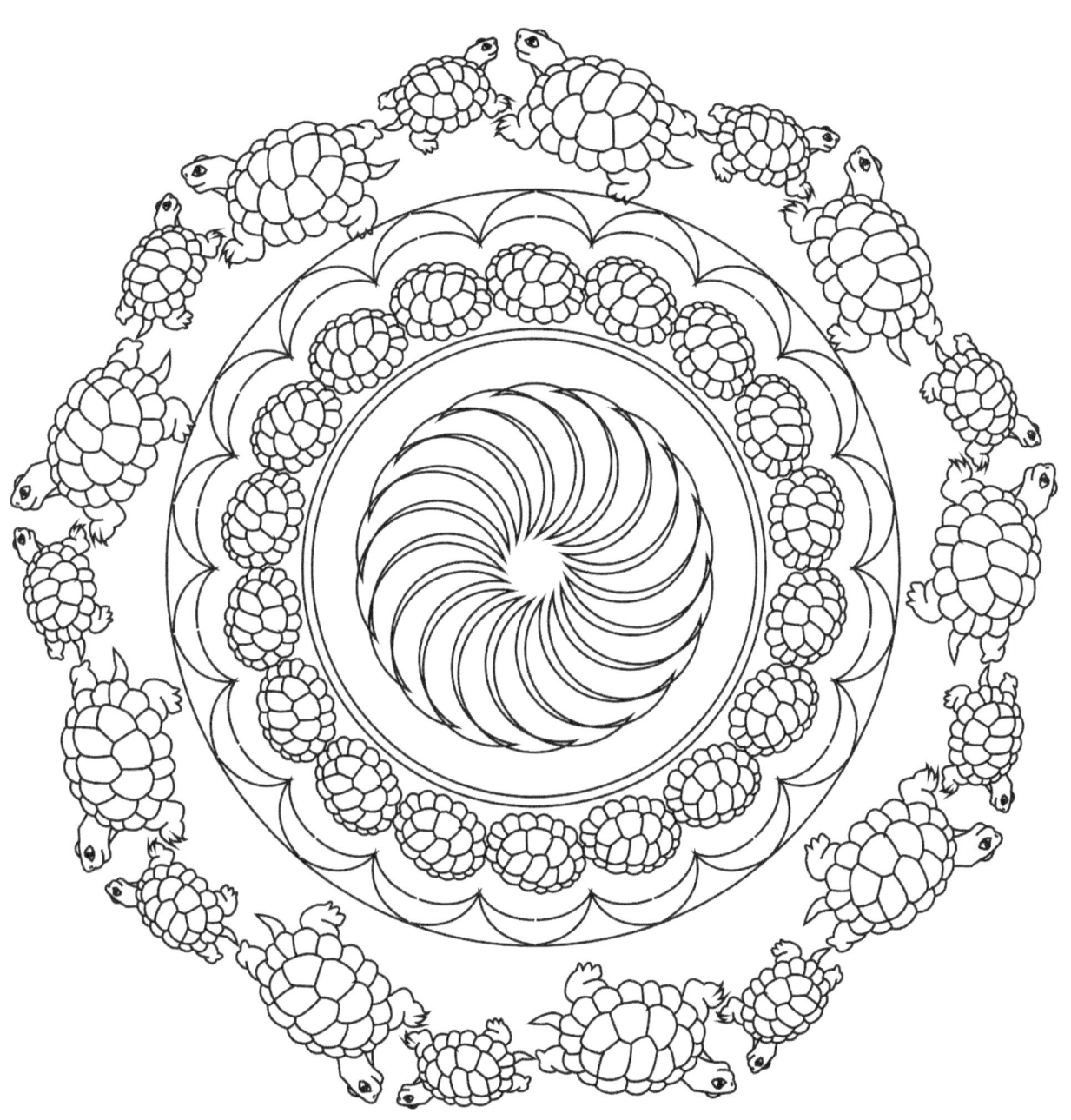

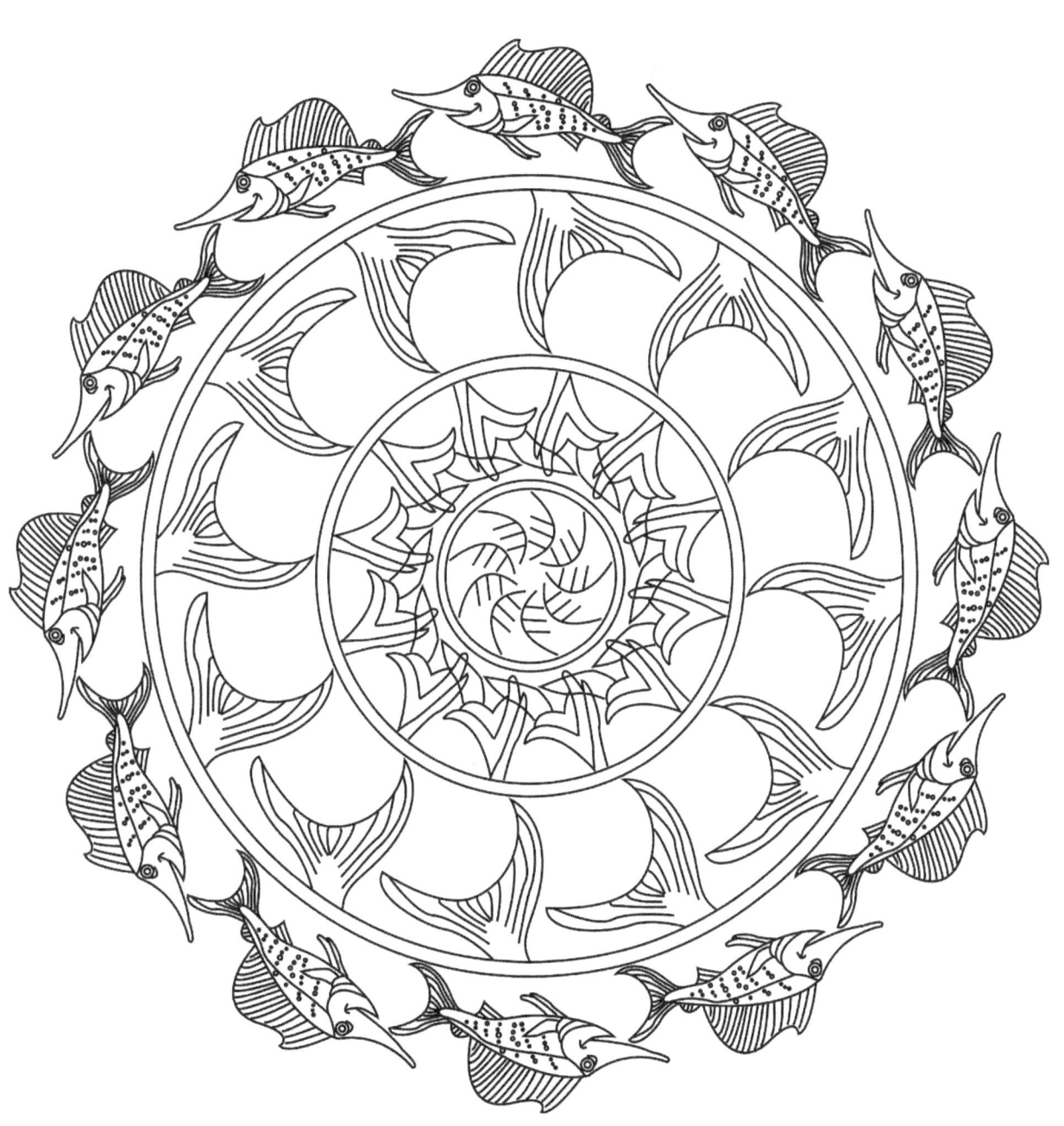

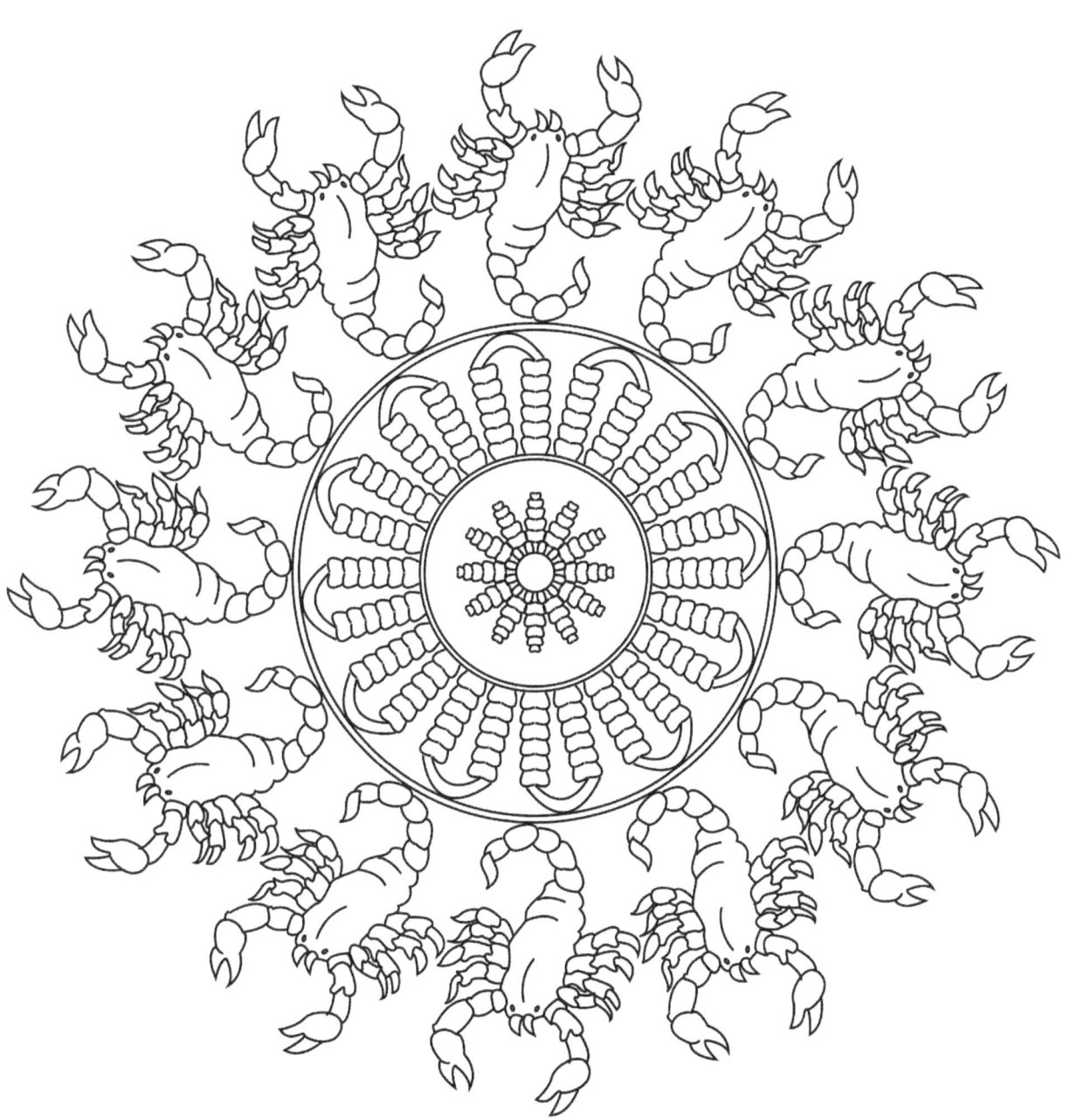

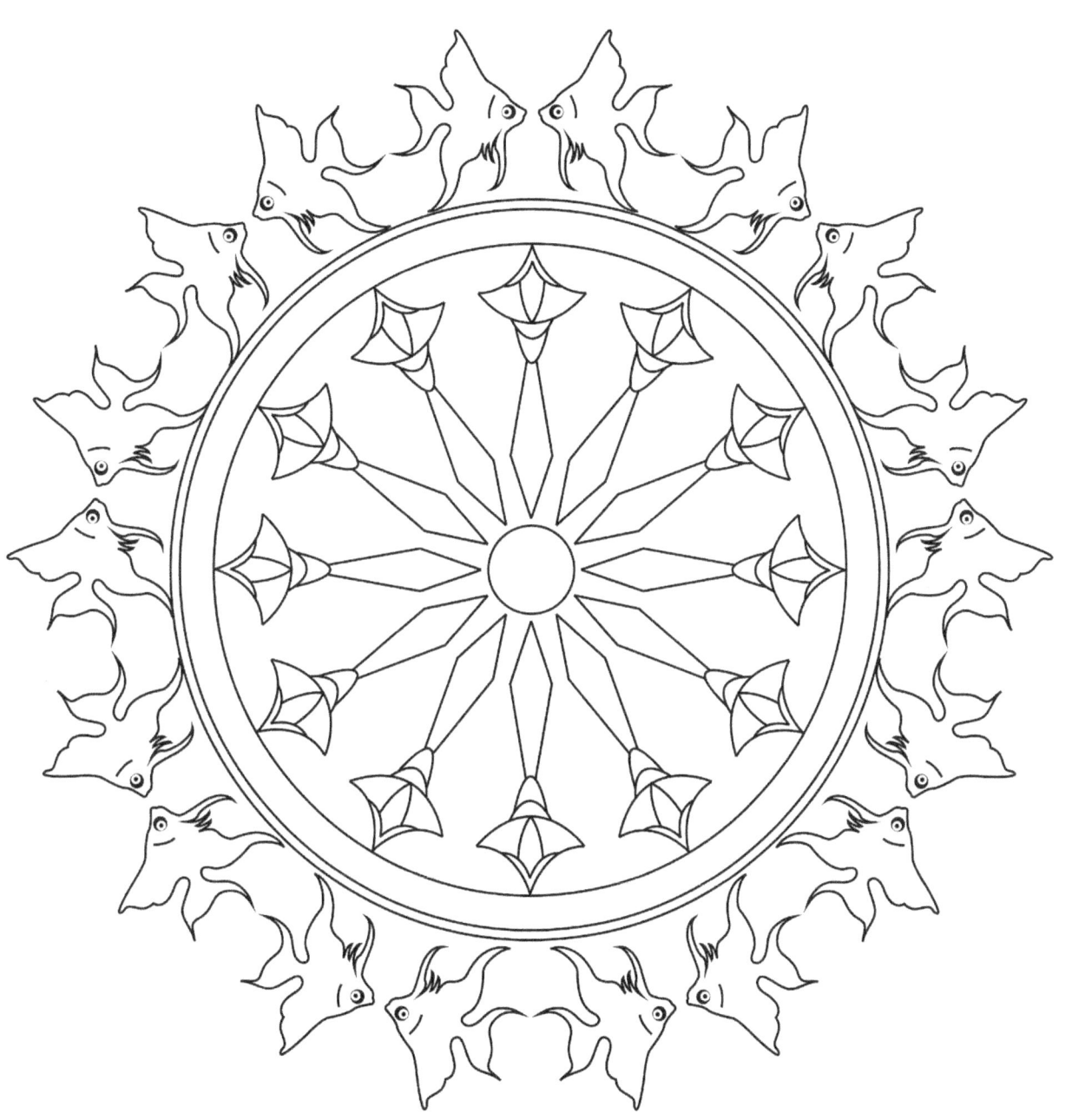

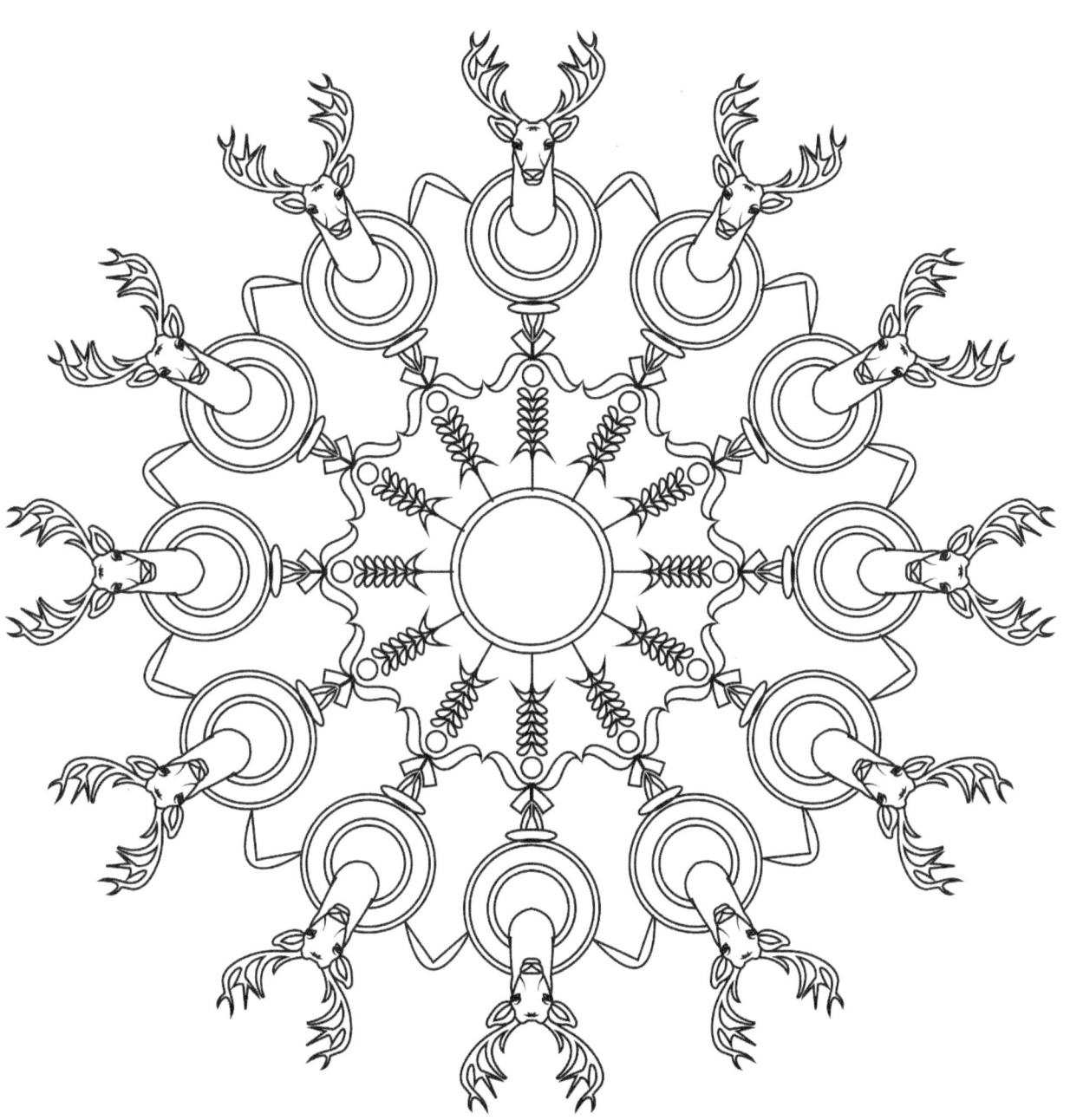

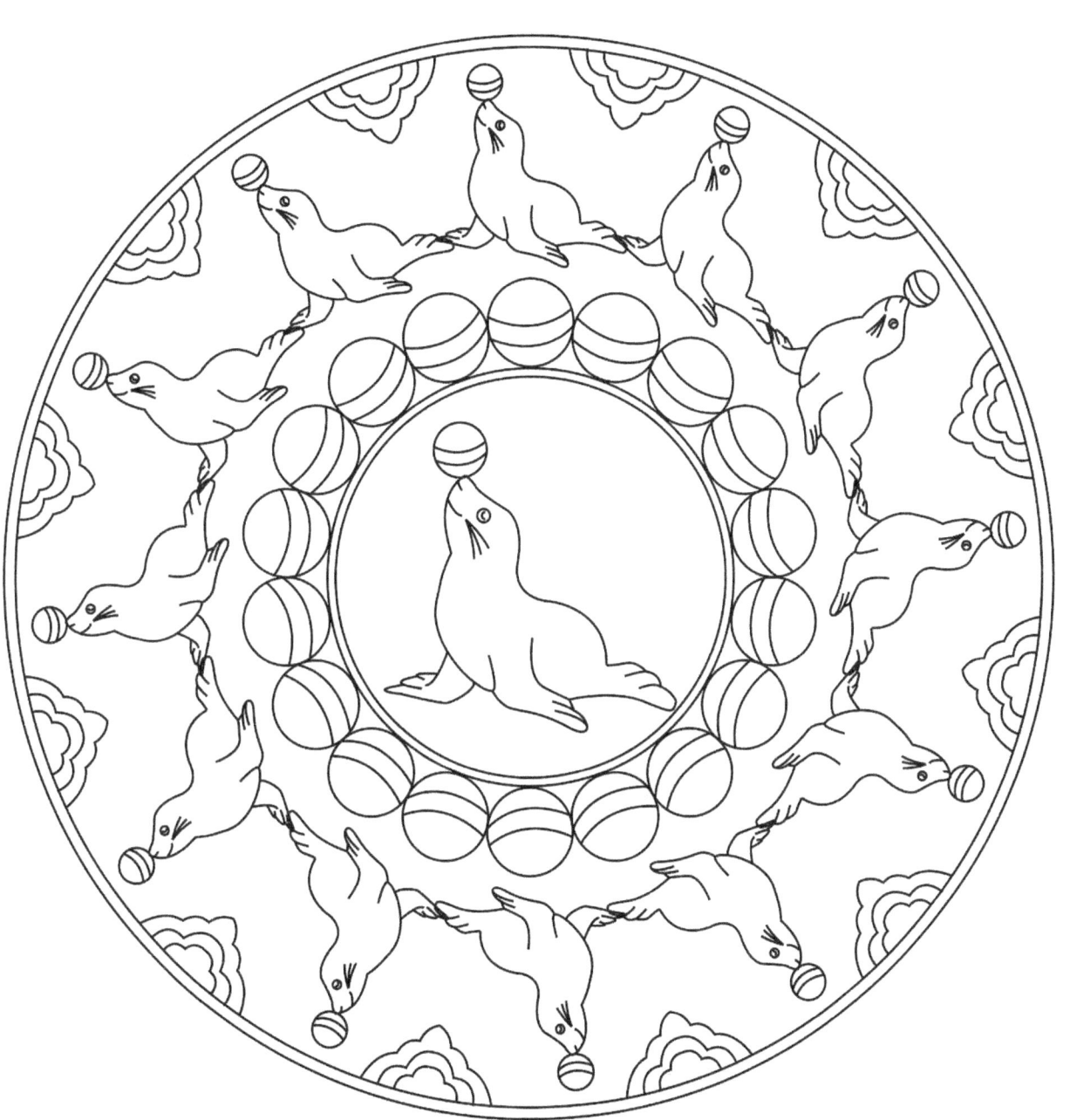

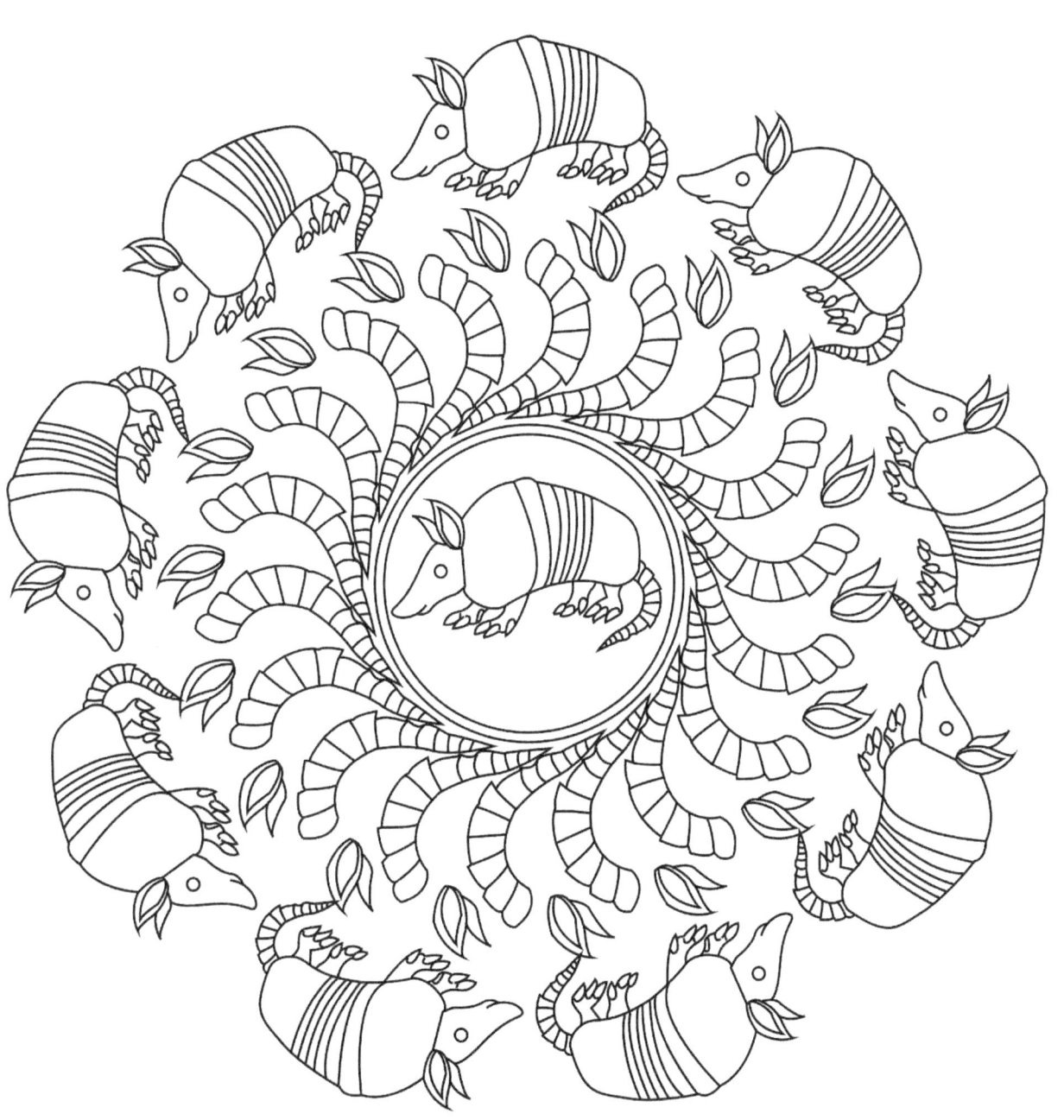

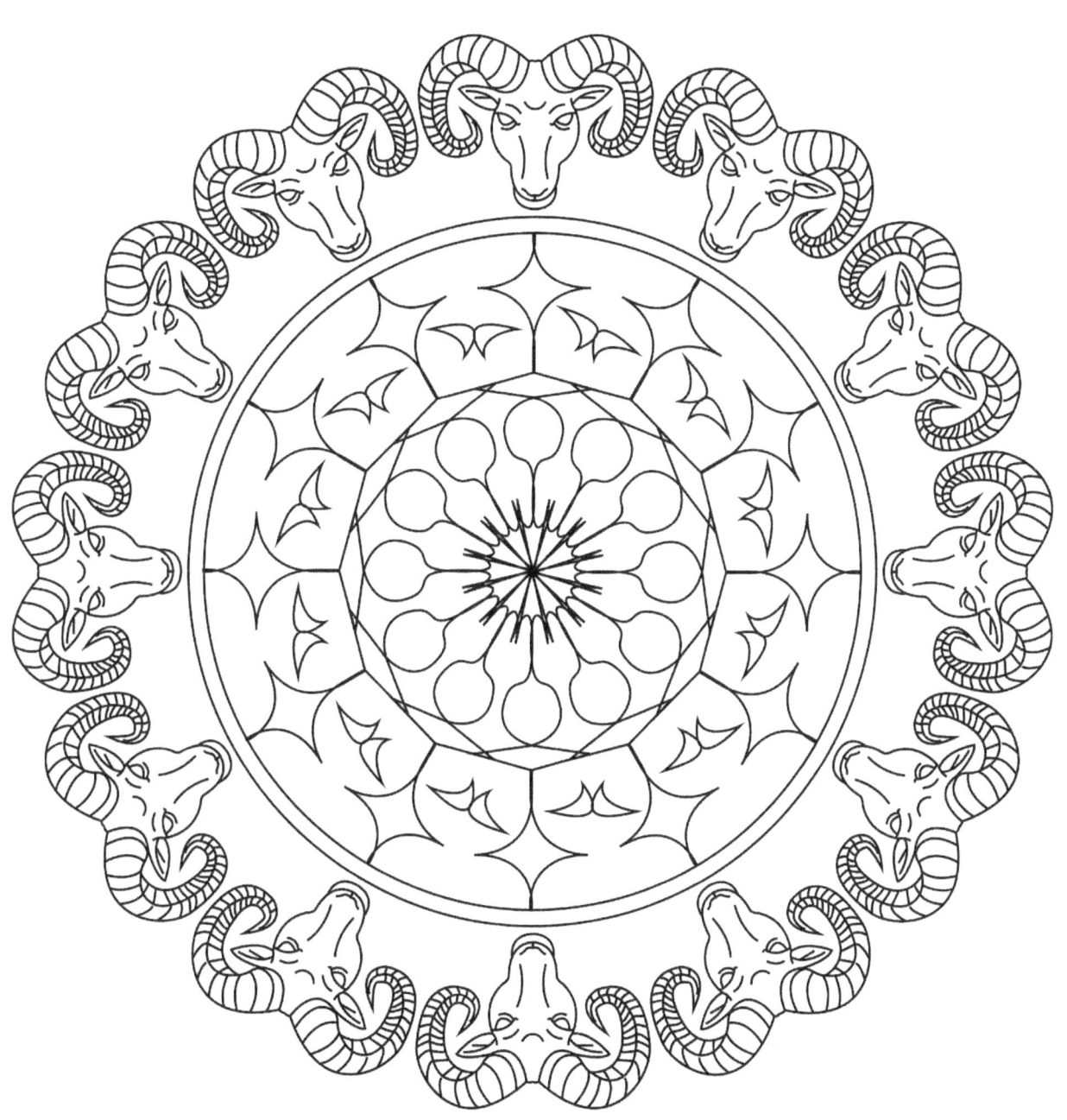

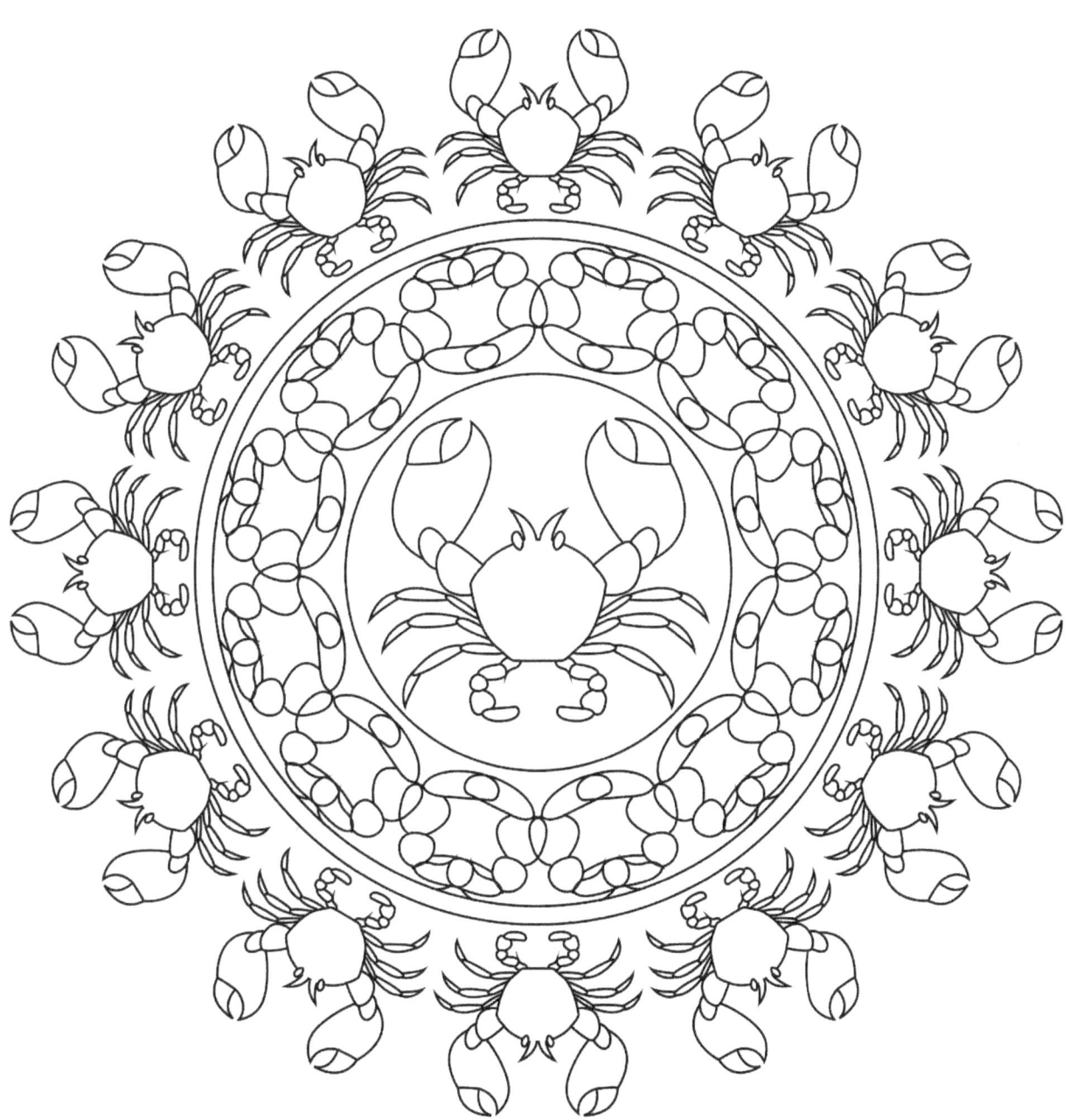

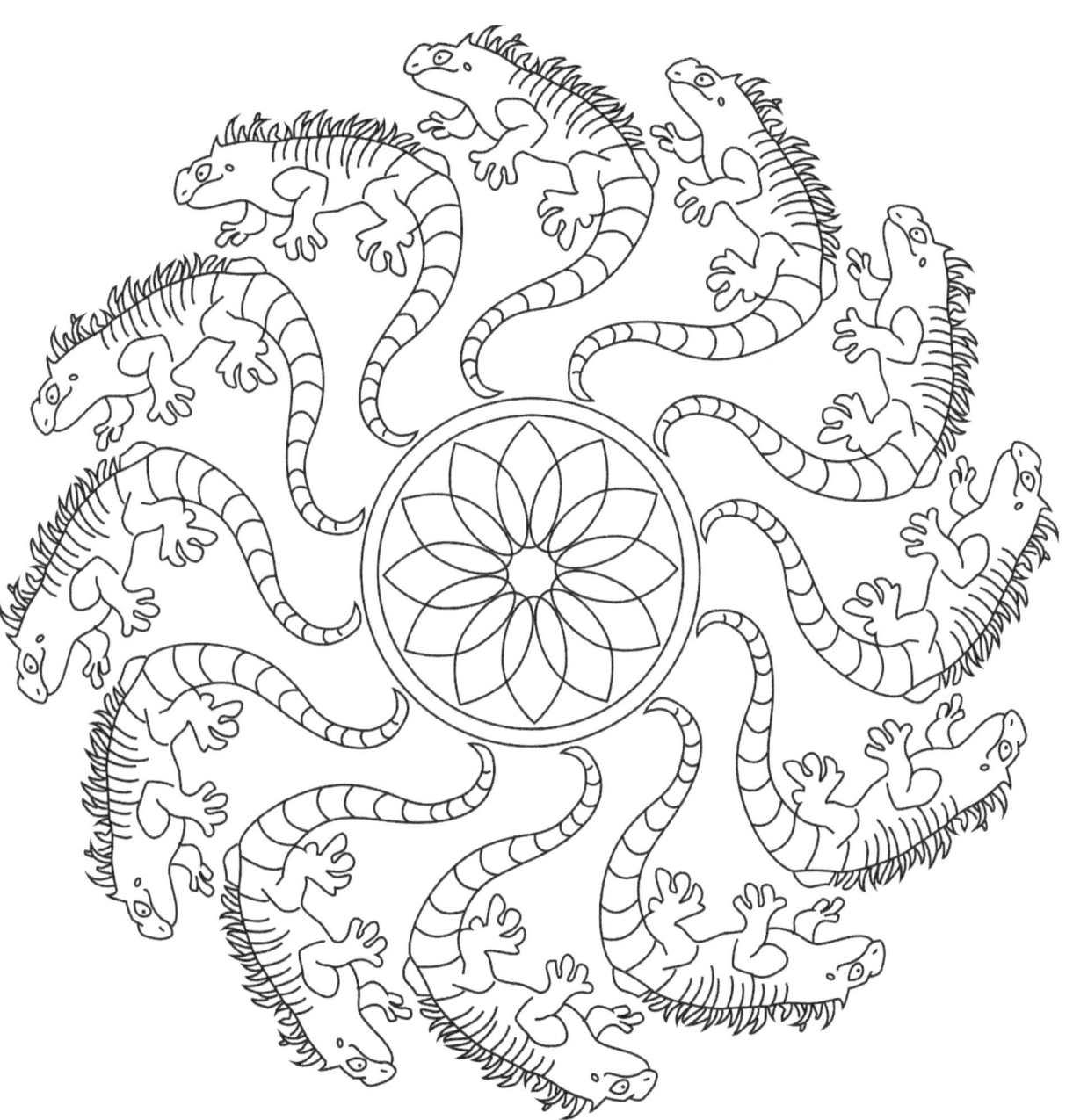

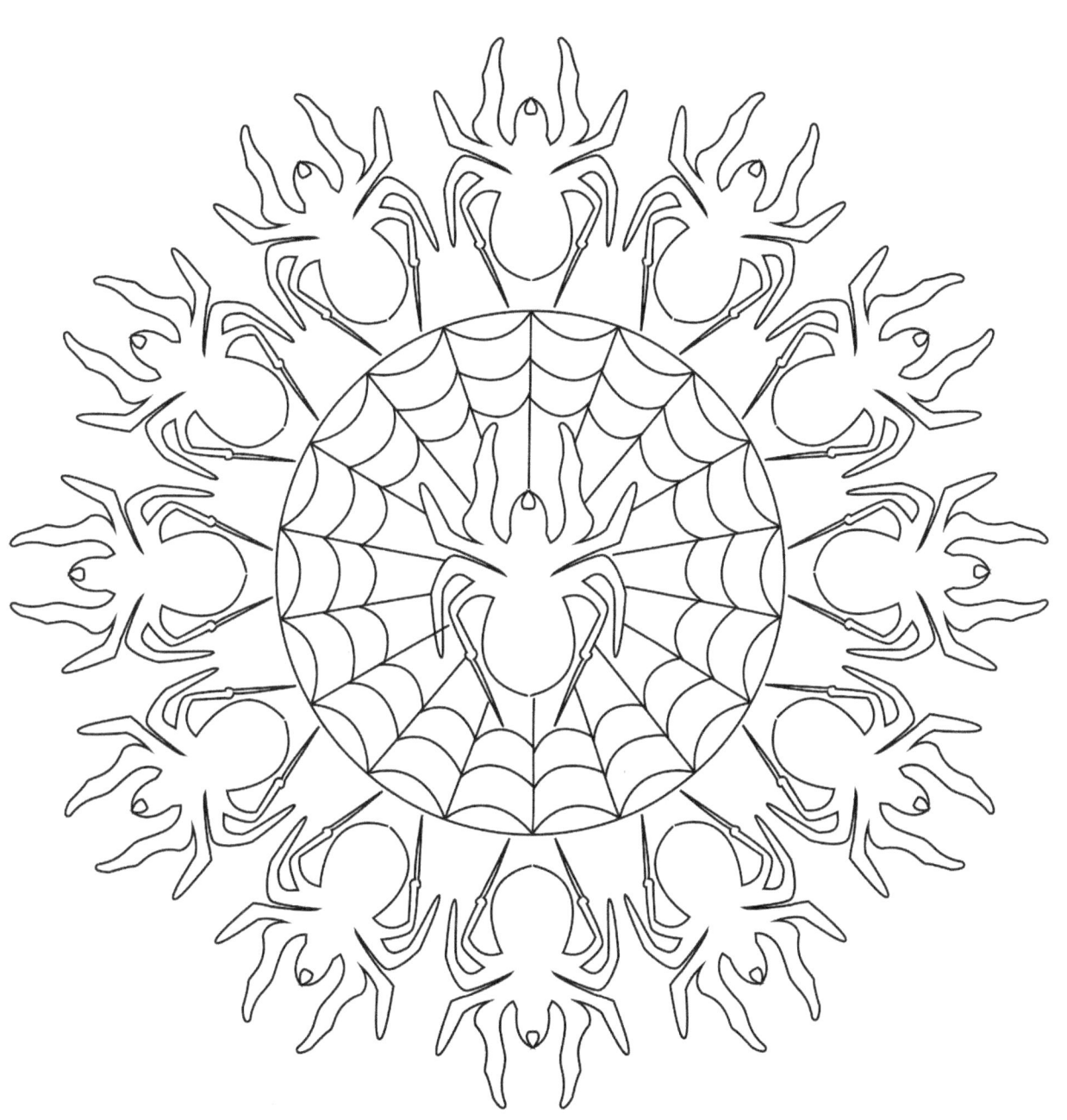

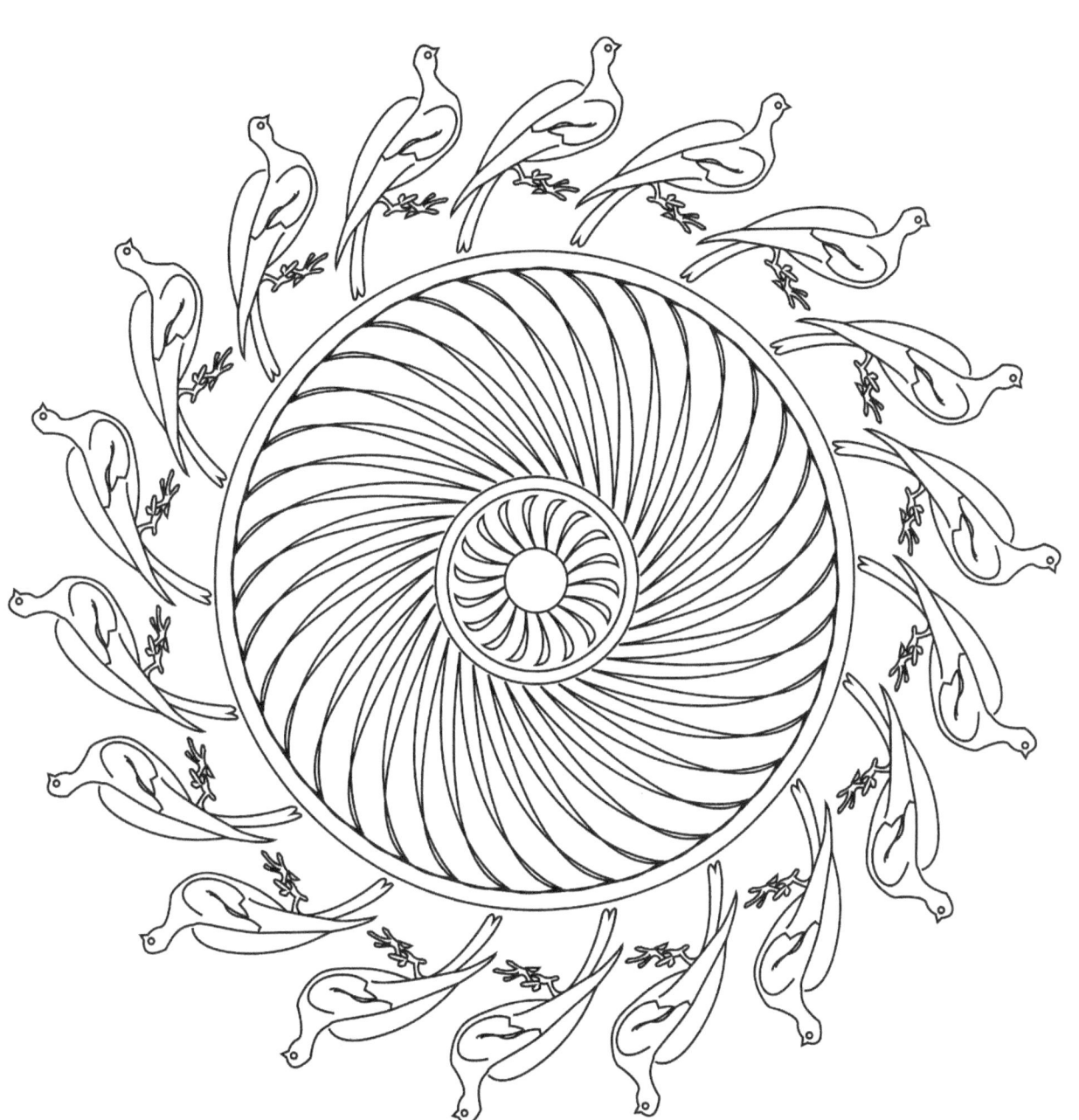

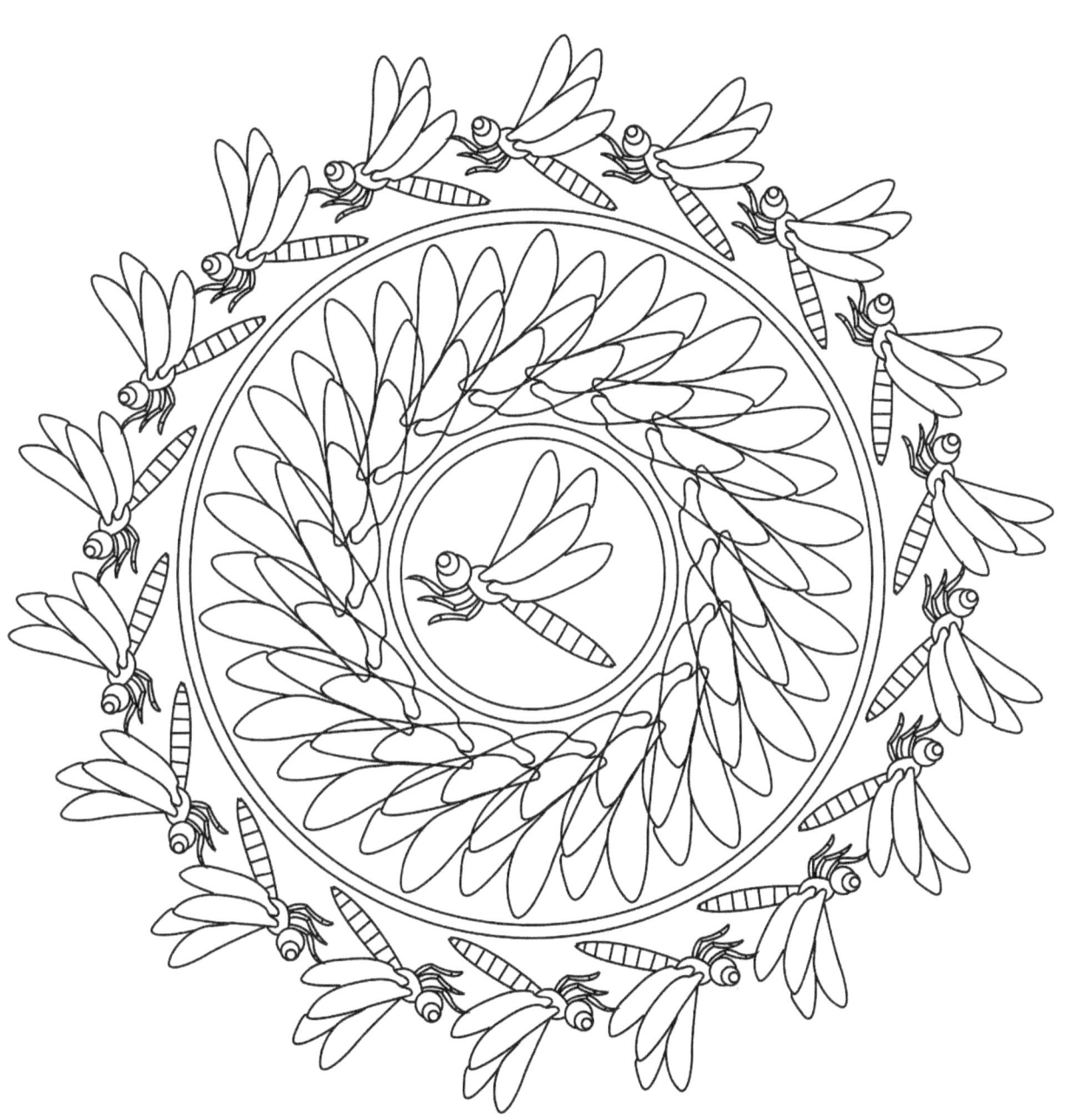

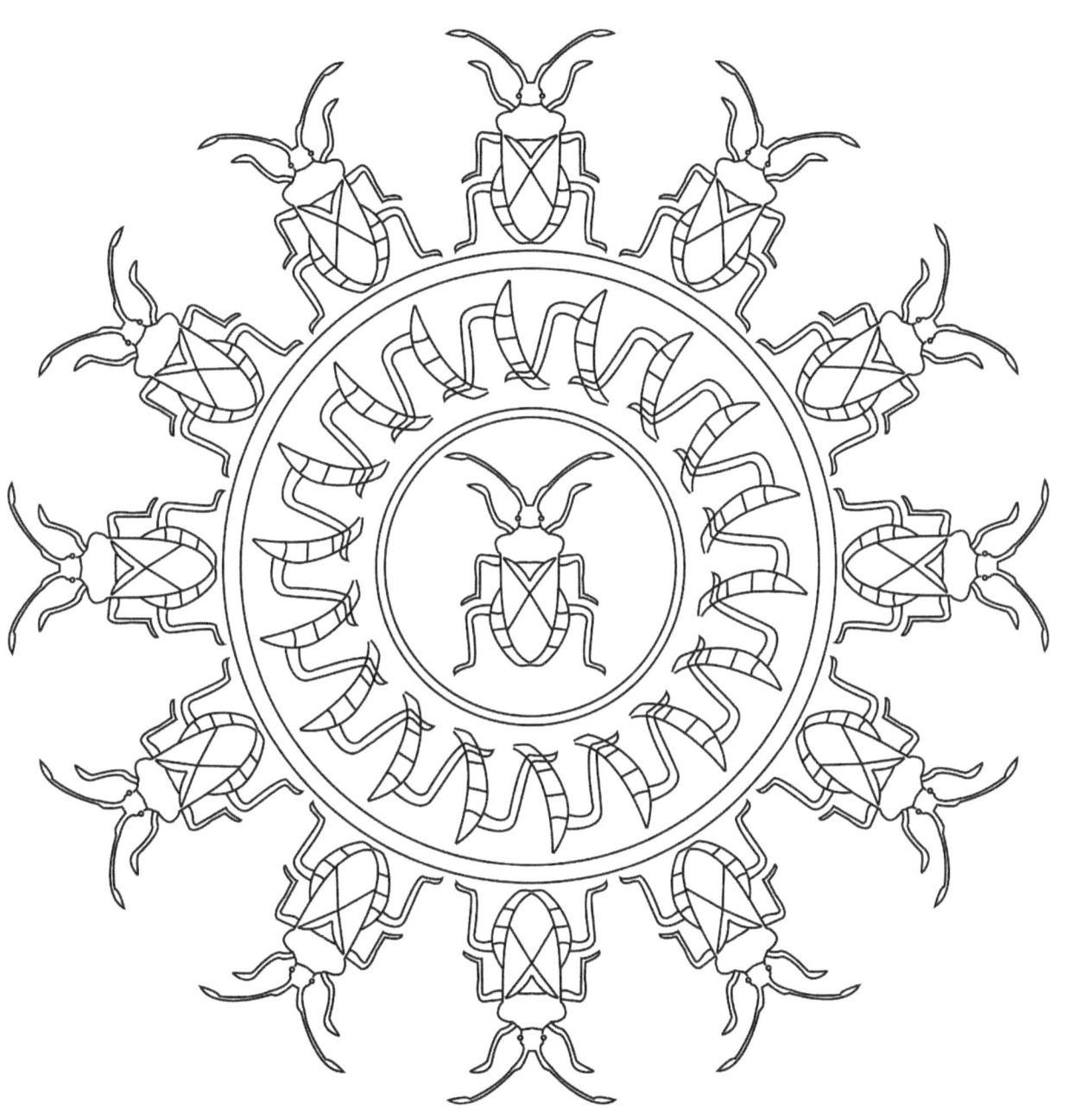